Reflections *on* Your Life

JOURNAL

REFLECTIVE LIVING SERIES

Reflections *on* Your Life

JOURNAL

*Discerning God's Voice in
the Everyday Moments of Life*

KEN GIRE

Chariot Victor Publishing
A Division of Cook Communications

Chariot Victor Publishing
A division of Cook Communications, Colorado Springs, Colorado 80918
Cook Communications, Paris, Ontario
Kingsway Communications, Eastbourne, England

REFLECTIONS ON YOUR LIFE
© 1998 by Ken Gire. Printed in the United States of America.
All rights reserved.

Editor: Greg Clouse
Cover Design: D² DesignWorks
Cover Photo: Tony Stone Images | David Muench

1 2 3 4 5 6 7 8 9 10 Printing/Year 02 01 00 99 98

Scripture quotations are from the *New American Standard Bible*, © the Lockman
Foundation 1960, 1962, 1963, 1968, 1971, 1972, 1973, 1975, 1977.

CONTENTS

This universal Voice of God was by the ancient Hebrews often called Wisdom, and was said to be everywhere sounding and searching throughout the earth, seeking some response from the sons of men. The eighth chapter of Proverbs begins, "Doth not wisdom cry? and understanding put forth her voice?" The writer then pictures wisdom as a beautiful woman standing "in the top of the high places, by the way in the places of the paths." She sounds her voice from every quarter so that no one may miss hearing it. "Unto you, O men, I call; and my voice is to the sons of men" (v. 4). Then she pleads for the simple and the foolish to give ear to her words. It is spiritual response for which this Wisdom of God is pleading, a response which she has always sought and is but rarely able to secure. The tragedy is that our eternal welfare depends upon our hearing, and we have trained our ears not to hear.

A.W. Tozer
The Pursuit of God

INTRODUCTION

In his journal of the time he spent at Walden Pond, Henry David Thoreau explained his reasons for going. "I went to the woods because I wished to live deliberately, to front only the essentials of life, and see if I could not learn what it had to teach, and not, when I came to die, discover that I had not lived."

The purpose of this journal is the same, to help us live deliberately, reducing life to its essentials in order to learn what it has to teach.

Why?

Because when our lives are over, none of us wants to look back and see only the time clock we've punched or the pages of the calendar we've torn off. We want more out of life than that. Thoreau certainly wanted more. In his journal he wrote, "I wanted to live deep and suck out all the marrow of life."

Isn't that what we all want? Isn't that what Jesus wants for us? Or what else could He have meant when He said, "I have come that you might have life and that you might have it abundantly"?

To experience life more abundantly, we are going to embark on an experiment similar to Thoreau's. Except we are not going into the woods to do it. We are going into *the world*. Our average, ordinary, workaday world. The world where an alarm starts the day. The world where during the day we all have to keep track of the time. And where at the end of the day we have to set the alarm and get things ready to do it all again tomorrow. It is the world where we all must go not only to make a living but somehow to make a life.

But how are we to make a life in such a world? How are we to learn what God has to teach us when the traffic in that world is so noisy? How are we to see God at work in our lives when our foot is heavy on the pedal and everything passes by in a blur? How are we to stop and be good Samaritans when our road to Jericho is a freeway?

How?

We do it in our world the same way Thoreau did it at Walden.

Deliberately.

We have to make some deliberate decisions to slow down on the roads we're traveling, to stop at the intersections, to look and to listen. We have to read the road signs, reflect on what they're saying, and respond. Sometimes that means getting off the freeway to take another way. Sometimes that means stopping to render aid to someone who needs help. Sometimes that means coming to a complete stop to avoid an accident.

Reflections on Your Life is designed to put a few speed bumps in our day, slowing us down long enough so we can read some of those signs.

Stop at those moments where you feel God may be speaking to you. Jot down what happened, whether it was a moment in the Scriptures or a moment at the grocery store. Whether it was a scene from a movie or something from a sermon. Whether it was an article in the morning paper or a story on the evening news. Something someone said . . . or didn't say.

Then take the time to reflect upon that moment. Respond in a prayerful way by reaching up to God, then in a personal way by reaching out to the people around you.

The journal will focus on topics aimed at heightening your awareness of such moments in your own life. To give resonance to the topics, I have quoted from some of the authors who have, through their books, served as mentors to me in learning to discern the voice of God in my own life. I hope the quotes will not only introduce you to some refreshing thinkers but also encourage you to investigate their writings more fully.

Although the topics are structured, it's important to understand that the moments are not. That's because the moments are spontaneous. We can prepare our heart to receive them, but we cannot plan when or where or how we will hear them. They cannot be predicted, only anticipated. And they cannot be manipulated. They can only be received or not received. That is our only choice.

This journal is a tool to help you become more receptive to those moments. To guide you along the way, I have written down some introductory thoughts at the beginning of each section followed by a moment in which I have sensed God leading me, prompting me, or speaking to me about my life.

Those moments have helped me realize that God is there, that He sees, that

He hears, that He cares. And that He is not silent. "He is," as A.W. Tozer said, "by His nature, continuously articulate. He fills the world with His speaking voice."

I hope this journal helps you hear that voice, especially the words He is speaking to you.

THE ART OF LISTENING

The idea of keeping a journal has for me always had a nagging, "you've-got-to-do-it-every-day" tone to it. To keep one at all, I've had to slip off the stiff shirt of that routine and slip into something with a little looser fit, allowing me to skip a few days here, a week there. But although that felt more comfortable, it didn't stop the nagging, which changed from "you've-got-to-do-it-every-day" to "you-need-to-catch-up."

More often than not, instead of keeping a journal, the journal kept me. Kept me feeling guilty mostly. My feelings changed, though, when instead of serving the journal, I used the journal to serve me. I kept it close to me but not chained to me. I wrote in it, not because I felt there was something I was supposed to say but because I felt there was something I was supposed to hear.

Sometimes what I heard was whispered, other times it was shouted. Sometimes it was a word, an image, or simply an impression. Sometimes the message was clear, other times it was obscure. As I started jotting down those moments, I began sensing that through some of those moments God was speaking.

In his autobiographical book, *The Sacred Journey*, Frederick Buechner writes: "If God speaks to us at all in this world, if God speaks anywhere, it is into our personal lives that he speaks. Someone we love dies, say. Some unforeseen act of kindness or cruelty touches the heart or makes the blood run cold. We fail a friend, or a friend fails us, and we are appalled at the capacity we all of us have for estranging the very people in our lives we need the most. Or maybe nothing extraordinary happens at all—just one day following another, helter-skelter, in the manner of days. We sleep and dream. We wake. We work. We remember and forget. And into the thick of it, or out of the thick of it, at moments of even the most humdrum of our days, God speaks."

Before we can hear God speaking through the everyday moments of our lives, our heart has to be prepared to listen. Which is more art than science. At least it has been that way for me. Preparing the heart in the art of listening involves several things.

First, there must be a sense of anticipation that God *wants* to speak to us and that He *will* speak. This anticipation stems from the belief that God is love and that it is the nature of love to express itself. The form of that expression, though, is remarkably varied. Sometimes love is expressed through words. Other times it is expressed through pictures or gestures or a variety of other ways, often very subtle ways that only the beloved might recognize. That is the nature of intimate communication. It is clear to the beloved but often cryptic to everyone else.

Second, there must be a humility of heart, for where we are willing to look and what we are willing to hear will largely determine how many of those moments we will catch. This posture of the heart stems from a belief that words from God characteristically come swaddled in the most lowly of appearances, and that if we're not willing to stoop, we'll likely miss God among the stench of the stable and the sweetness of the straw.

Third, there must be a responsiveness to what is heard. A willingness to follow where we are being led, wherever that may be. A readiness to admit where we are wrong and to align ourselves with what is right and good and true. An eagerness to enter into the joy of the moment. Or into the sorrow of the moment, if that's the case. It is this responsiveness of the heart that makes us susceptible to the grace of the moment. And it is what prepares us to receive whatever grace is offered to us in the next.

How to Use This guided Journal

You may use this journal in a couple of different ways:

1. You may prefer to write your moments in the sections in which they are emphasized. For example, if you sense God has spoken to you in prayer, record your thoughts using a blank entry in that section. The fact that this approach is more subject oriented than daily oriented allows you the flexibility to flip from one section to another if that is what you prefer.

2. You may prefer to be more spontaneous, journaling your moments from one undated entry to the next regardless of the focus of the section. For example, you may journal about a special moment God spoke to you through nature even though you are in the section on prayer.

Note: Since the "Moments" sections are not exhaustive of the kinds you may experience, an "Open Topic Section" has been included at the back of the journal.

Whatever your method, remember the goal of this journal is to help you establish habits of the heart that nurture a more reflective life.

MOMENTS OF EVERYDAY LIFE

When God created the earth, it was a magnificent ecosystem for all the life He placed there. For the creatures that dwelt in the oceans. For those that dwelt in the skies. And for those that dwelt on the land.

As a dwelling for man, the masterpiece of creation, God designed a special place. A garden. It was an architectural triumph of both form and function, for it not only provided food and shelter for the body, it provided beauty and refreshment for the soul.

But the garden was designed to be more than a place to meet man's physical and spiritual needs. It was designed to be the ideal environment for God to cultivate His relationship with man. It was designed not only to be a bountiful place and a beautiful place, but a quiet place.

A place conducive for reflection.

Like an art gallery.

The garden was a place through which the man and woman could leisurely stroll, stopping to note the intricate design of a leaf . . . then moving on until another display stopped them, this time the exquisite colors in an orchid . . . then strolling a little farther until they came upon the branching grandeur of a tree.

The displays must have prompted questions. Who is the Artist responsible for these things? What is He like? How can we know Him?

The psalmist says that the heavens continually reveal the breathless artistry of God, that "day to day pours forth speech, and night to night reveals knowledge" (Psalm 19:1-2). Yet, as the psalmist informs us, the style of the revelation is subtle. "There is no speech, nor are there words; their voice is not heard" (v. 3).

Like an art historian walking us through the gallery, the psalmist tells us the beginning principles for understanding what we see. Whatever it is the Artist is trying to say, He is saying it through pictures not words.

If that is true, it stands to reason that the garden where man was placed was full of pictures that revealed something of who God is, what He values, how He works. Looking at some of the pictures, we can see a few of those things.

He is an *artistic* God, whose palette ranges from the most muted of colors to the most magnificent. His panache can be seen in the peacock. His plainness, in the sparrow.

He is a *powerful* God, who created tall and stately redwoods. He is also a gentle God, who delicately dotted the backs of ladybugs.

He is an *orderly* God, who values process—first the stalk, then the leaf, then the blossom, then the fruit. Yet within the creative order, there is an almost playful spontaneity. You see it in the wind that tussles a towheaded dandelion. You see it in the whimsical twitch of a squirrel's tail. You see it in the prism of colors that sparkles from a dewdrop.

In the same way the creation reveals knowledge, so do the circumstances of our lives. The moment-by-moment events of our lives fall into the soil of our understanding like seeds. Our responsibility, like that of our first parents, is to work the garden. To prepare the soil. To tend the growth. And to take what is offered from its branches as nourishment for our soul.

Date *Oct. 10, 1997*

Every moment and every event of every man's life on earth plants something in his soul. For just as the wind carries thousands of invisible and visible winged seeds, so the stream of time brings with it germs of spiritual vitality that come to rest imperceptibly in the minds and wills of men. Most of these unnumbered seeds perish and are lost, because men are not prepared to receive them.

Thomas Merton
Seeds of Contemplation

REFLECTING ON YOUR LIFE

Reading the Moment

Sports page of USA Today. Cover story headline reads: "Smith ignores pleas, tearfully steps down." It was the press release of Dean Smith's retirement from college basketball. At 66, he is ending a 36-year career. In those 36 years, he amassed 879 wins, 2 NCAA championships, 11 trips to the final four, and a graduation rate for his players of 97.3%. The article included quotes from his players and other coaches and fans, but it was a quote from him that caused me to pause and reflect. While watching Larry Brown running the 76er's training camp at the North Carolina Dean Dome, Smith said: "Larry Brown always fires me up. I used to be like that. If I can't give this team that enthusiasm, I said I would get out. That's honestly how I feel."

Reflecting on the Moment

I've always enjoyed basketball, whether it's playing the game or watching it. No matter how busy my schedule is, I always make room for the final four at the end of March. Many of those final four games featured North Carolina, coached by Dean Smith. Like his fans, I was sorry to see him leave, but the reason he left made me respect him all the more. He didn't leave because the basketball program was in shambles and would take years to rebuild. He left because the passion he once had for the game had left him. And he knew that without that passion, he couldn't give his best. His players deserved better, he thought. So did the fans. He left, to everyone's surprise. But he left with everyone's respect.

Is there any passage of Scripture that comes to mind that sheds light on this moment?

A good name is to be more desired than great riches (Proverbs)

Responding to the Moment

Reaching up prayerfully

Father, please help me to have passion for what I do as a writer. And when the passion is gone, give me the courage and strength and integrity of a Dean Smith to make the decision to step aside so room will be made for someone who has that passion.

Reaching out personally

I'm feeling my passion waning lately. Too many commitments. Too few pauses in my life. I can't do much about it right now, but I am determined to be more careful about my schedule, because what gets crowded out in the end, is my passion for living, for writing, for other people, and for God. Judy and I have set aside Sat. mornings to go out for breakfast & talk. That's been good, and, something I look forward to all week.

In humility, receive the word implanted, which is able to save your souls. (*James 1:21*)

Date

Redwoods are the largest and tallest living creatures. The trees among which I live some-times reach three hundred and sixty feet to sweep the sun's rays from the sky. They are babies at a hundred years, adolescent at five hundred and mature around a thousand years of age. The rings on fallen trees reveal that some of them have lived twenty-five hundred years. . . . The most astounding fact of all is that these trees spring from seeds so tiny that it takes three to six thousand of them to weigh an ounce.

Morton Kelsey
Prayer & The Redwood Seed

REFLECTING ON YOUR LIFE

Reading the Moment

Reflecting on the Moment

Is there any passage of Scripture that comes to mind that sheds light on this moment?

Responding to the Moment

Reaching up prayerfully

Reaching out personally

The kingdom of heaven is like a mustard seed, which a man took and sowed in his field; and this is smaller than all other seeds; but when it is full grown, it is larger than the garden plants, and becomes a tree, so that the birds of the air come and nest in its branches. (*Matthew 13:31-32*)

Date

Though I do not believe that a plant will spring up where no seed has been, I have great faith in a seed. Convince me that you have a seed there, and I am prepared to expect wonders.

Henry David Thoreau
The Dispersion of Seeds

REFLECTING ON YOUR LIFE

Reading the Moment

Reflecting on the Moment

Is there any passage of Scripture that comes to mind that sheds light on this moment?

Responding to the Moment

Reaching up prayerfully

Reaching out personally

For you have been born again not of seed which is perishable but imperishable, that is, through the living and abiding word of God. (*1 Peter 1:23*)

Date

The sower went out to sow his seed; and as he sowed, some fell beside the road; and it was trampled under foot, and the birds of the air ate it up. And other seed fell on rocky soil, and as soon as it grew up, it withered away, because it had no moisture. And other seed fell among the thorns; and the thorns grew up with it, and choked it out. And other seed fell into the good soil, and grew up, and produced a crop a hundred times as great.

(Luke 8:5-8)

REFLECTING ON YOUR LIFE

Reading the Moment

Reflecting on the Moment

Is there any passage of Scripture that comes to mind that sheds light on this moment?

Responding to the Moment

Reaching up prayerfully

Reaching out personally

Now the parable is this: the seed is the word of God. And those beside the road are those who have heard; then the devil comes and takes away the word from their heart, so that they may not believe and be saved. And those on the rocky soil are those who, when they hear, receive the word with joy; and these have no firm root; they believe for a while, and in time of temptation fall away. And the seed which fell among the thorns, these are the ones who have heard, and as they go on their way they are choked with worries and riches and pleasures of this life, and bring no fruit to maturity. And the seed in the good soil, these are the ones who have heard the word in an honest and good heart, and hold it fast, and bear fruit with perseverance. (*Luke 8:11-15*)

Date

A man's mind may be likened to a garden, which may be intelligently cultivated or allowed to run wild; but whether cultivated or neglected, it must, and will, *bring forth*. If no useful seeds are put into it, then an abundance of useless weed-seeds will *fall* therein, and will continue to produce their kind.

Just as a gardener cultivates his plot, keeping it free from weeds, and growing the flowers and fruits which he requires, so may a man tend the garden of his mind, weeding out all the wrong, useless, and impure thoughts, and cultivating toward perfection the flowers and fruits of right, useful, and pure thoughts.

James Allen
As a Man Thinketh

REFLECTING ON YOUR LIFE

Reading the Moment

Reflecting on the Moment

Is there any passage of Scripture that comes to mind that sheds light on this moment?

Responding to the Moment

Reaching up prayerfully

Reaching out personally

I passed by the field of the sluggard, and by the vineyard of the man lacking sense; and behold, it was completely overgrown with thistles, its surface was covered with nettles, and its stone wall was broken down. When I saw, I reflected upon it; I looked, and received instruction. "A little sleep, a little slumber, a little folding of the hands to rest," then your poverty will come as a robber, and your want like an armed man. (*Proverbs 24:30-34*)

Date

All creatures live by the hand of God. The senses can only grasp the work of man, but faith sees the work of divine action in everything. It sees that Jesus Christ lives in all things, extending his influence over the centuries so that the briefest moment and the tiniest atom contain a portion of that hidden life and its mysterious work. Jesus Christ, after his resurrection, surprised the disciples when he appeared before them in disguise, only to vanish as soon as he had declared himself. The same Jesus still lives and works among us, still surprises souls whose faith is not sufficiently pure and strong. There is no moment when God is not manifest in the form of some affliction, obligation or duty. Everything that happens to us, in us, and through us, embraces and conceals God's divine but veiled purpose, so that we are always being taken by surprise and never recognize it until it has been accomplished. If we could pierce the veil and if we were vigilant and attentive, God would unceasingly reveal himself to us and we would rejoice in his works and all that happens to us. We would say to everything: "It is the Lord!"

Jean-Pierre De Caussade
The Sacrament of the Present Moment

REFLECTING ON YOUR LIFE

Reading the Moment

Reflecting on the Moment

Is there any passage of Scripture that comes to mind that sheds light on this moment?

Responding to the Moment

Reaching up prayerfully

Reaching out personally

But Mary was standing outside the tomb weeping; and so, as she wept, she stooped and looked into the tomb; and she beheld two angels in white sitting, one at the head, and one at the feet, where the body of Jesus had been lying. And they said to her, "Woman, why are you weeping?"

She said to them, "Because they have taken away my Lord, and I do not know where they have laid Him." When she had said this, she turned around, and beheld Jesus standing there, and did not know that it was Jesus.

Jesus said to her, "Woman, why are you weeping? Whom are you seeking?"

Supposing Him to be the gardener, she said to Him, "Sir, if you have carried Him away, tell me where you have laid Him, and I will take Him away."

Jesus said to her, "Mary!"

She turned and said to Him in Hebrew, "Rabboni!" (which means, Teacher).

Jesus said to her, "Stop clinging to Me, for I have not yet ascended to the Father; but go to My brethren, and say to them, 'I ascend to My Father and your Father, and My God and your God.'"

Mary Magdalene came, announcing to the disciples, "I have seen the Lord," and that He had said these things to her. (*John 20:11-18*)

MOMENTS IN PRAYER

I don't usually hear God speaking when I pray. That is probably because more often than not I am talking when I should be listening. Prattling in the presence of God, is the way Dietrich Bonhoeffer puts it in his book, *Life Together*.

I think it's more of a Protestant shortcoming, this prattling. An obsessive need to fill the silences in our lives. As if wordless spaces were somehow wasted spaces. Or as if we feared the silences the way a child fears the dark, afraid some shadowy figure will come out of hiding to do who knows what terrible things to us. So we whistle in the dark, filling the silences with our words.

Whether what we fear from them is something as simple as wastefulness or as sinister as what may be lurking in the closets of our subconscious, the silences are not to be feared. For it is in the silences that God most often speaks.

If that is true, it stands to reason that we increase our odds of hearing what He has to say if we still our soul, calm our heart, quiet the yammering of our own inner voices. And wait.

This waiting silence is a biblical pattern for hearing God. Eli told Samuel how to hear God's voice, which at first was unfamiliar to the young boy, when the priest counseled him to call out into the night with the words, "Speak, Lord, for Thy servant is listening" (1 Samuel 3:9). David tried to bring about this receptive stillness within himself when he said, "My soul, wait in silence for God only" (Psalm 62:5). And Jeremiah advised the person seeking God, "It is good that he waits silently for the salvation of the Lord" (Lamentations 3:26).

But though the pattern is a biblical one, it is by no means a natural one. Our natural tendencies are restive, not reflective. As Henri Nouwen said in *Reaching Out*, "We always seem to have something more urgent to do and 'just sitting there' and 'doing nothing' often disturbs us more than it helps. But there is no way around this. Being useless and silent in the presence of our God belongs to the core of all prayer. In the beginning we often hear our own unruly noises more loudly than God's voice. This is at times very hard to tolerate. But slowly, very slowly, we discover that the silent time makes us quiet and deepens our awareness of ourselves and God. Then, very soon, we start missing these moments when we are deprived of them, and before we are fully aware of it an inner momentum has developed that draws us more and more into silence and closer to that still point where God speaks to us."

Prayer is most often thought of as a time for us to speak with God. But it is also, I think, a time for God to speak with us. Sometimes He speaks with articulate clarity. Other times, with groanings too deep for words, speaking from His Spirit to ours in the form of some inner conviction. He may not respond immediately. He may answer later in the day or later in our life, for His sense of urgency is different from ours.

There are moments in prayer, however, when God *does* speak. As in any conversation, though, unless we pause to listen, we're likely to miss it. As you take time during the week to pray, try talking less and listening more. It is of course possible you won't hear anything. But if you're not listening, it's certain you won't.

Date *End of January, 1998*

All who have walked with God have viewed prayer as the main business of their lives.

Richard Foster

Celebration of Discipline

REFLECTING ON YOUR LIFE

Reading the Moment

I was scheduled to speak at a youth worker's banquet on February 3rd in Colorado Springs. I had known about the event for 2 months and had something already planned, but I prayed repeatedly that if God wanted something else said than what I had planned to say that He would somehow let me know. A few days before the banquet, He did. I had a dream, and in that dream I was speaking to a male youth leader who was fairly young himself. He was telling me how much he loved God and kids, but how afraid he was of sex and the possibility of getting involved with someone in his ministry. He was trembling when he told me this, and then he asked, "Will you help me? Please."

Reflecting on the Moment

It seemed to me, since I had been praying for God's guidance for sometime now concerning what to speak about, that this is what He wanted me to speak about. I wasn't totally sure, but I was more sure about going in that direction than the one I had originally planned. I thought about my days as a youth worker and the temptations I struggled with. I thought about some of my friends who weren't so fortunate in extricating themselves from temptation as I had been, and even then only barely had I been, by luck or circumstance or the good grace of God. So I began thinking and studying and praying about what I should say to them about this subject of sexual temptation.

Is there any passage of Scripture that comes to mind that sheds light on this moment?

Proverbs 7 and 8 about the ~~adulter~~ adulterous woman.
Watch over your heart with all diligence for from it flows the issues of life – Prov. 4:23. See also Mk. 7:14-23 Sin starts in the heart. Also Mt. 5:27-8 Adultery begins in the heart.

Responding to the Moment

Reaching up prayerfully

Dear God, help me to speak what you would want said at that youth workers luncheon. Help me find the words that would in some way help them with the struggle that we all have over sex. Help me to go there to serve them. They all work so very hard and for such little pay. Help my words to be of some encouragement and refreshment to them all.

Reaching out personally

Decided to use 2 clips from the movie Camelot, one to show how innocently an affair can begin; the other, to show how devastating it can be in the end. There's an image of a candle in the movie that symbolizes the first flame of ~~their~~ Guenevere's love for Lancelot. Use candle as an illustration. Also some verses from Proverbs. Example of David & Bathsheba.

And in the early morning, while it was still dark, He arose and went out and departed to a lonely place, and was praying there. (*Mark 1:35*)

Date

Jacob looked down his path as if it were the current of a great river. As he stared into the flow he saw the seemingly unending line of moments given to him. Then, like a man marking a trail, he began to put his prayer between the moments, making the common profound by pausing.

Using prayer to tie knots in time, Jacob isolated the details that would pass before others as a stream of events.

In this way Jacob secured the moments in his life, returned their individuality, allowed the luster in each of them to be observed, and, appreciated and saved, transformed his moments into a string of pearls.

Noah benShea
Jacob's Journey

REFLECTING ON YOUR LIFE

Reading the Moment

Reflecting on the Moment

Is there any passage of Scripture that comes to mind that sheds light on this moment?

Responding to the Moment

Reaching up prayerfully

Reaching out personally

Pray without ceasing; in everything give thanks; for this is God's will for you in Christ Jesus. (*1 Thessalonians 5:17-18*)

Date

Prayer is a two-way conversation between man and God! It is no mere monologue; it is a dialogue. Prayer is a double search: God reaching down toward man, and man reaching up toward God, each straining toward the other like the two immense figures of God and Adam which Michelangelo painted on the ceiling of the Sistine Chapel.

Kenneth Eaton
Men Who Talked with God

REFLECTING ON YOUR LIFE

Reading the Moment

Reflecting on the Moment

Is there any passage of Scripture that comes to mind that sheds light on this moment?

Responding to the Moment

Reaching up prayerfully

Reaching out personally

I love the Lord because He hears
My voice and my supplications.
Because He has inclined His ear to me,
Therefore I shall call upon Him as long as I live.
(*Psalm 116:1-2*)

My sheep hear My voice, and I know them, and they follow Me. (*John 10:27*)

Date

Listen to your heart. It's there that Jesus speaks most intimately to you. Praying is first and foremost listening to Jesus, who dwells in the very depths of your heart. He doesn't shout. He doesn't thrust himself upon you. His voice is an unassuming voice, very nearly a whisper, the voice of a gentle love.

Henri Nouwen
Way of the Heart

REFLECTING ON YOUR LIFE

Reading the Moment

Reflecting on the Moment

Is there any passage of Scripture that comes to mind that sheds light on this moment?

Responding to the Moment

Reaching up prayerfully

Reaching out personally

Behold, I stand at the door and knock; if anyone hears My voice and opens the door, I will come in to him, and will dine with him, and he with Me. (*Revelation 3:20*)

Date

Why should God bother to take Abraham into his confidence? He seems to feel a sense of obligation toward Abraham. Why? If you think about it for a moment you will realize the stupendous implication of the story. The Lord of far-flung galaxies, the Creator of life and of all that exists, the All-Powerful, the All-Knowing, the Inscrutable, the Judge of angels, demons and people is taking the trouble to explain his actions to an individual, and is talking without condescension, but in terms that he can understand. . . .

It may seem inconceivable that the same God wants such a relationship with you. You are a creature he made. You are a sinner he redeemed. You are even his child by adoption and by supernatural new birth. Yet he calls you to a higher dignity—to that of friend and partner. . . .

Two facts necessarily follow. If you are his friend, he will share his thoughts and plans with you. If you are his partner, he will be concerned about your views on his plans and projects. Whatever else prayer may be, it is intended to be a sharing and a taking counsel with God on matters of importance to him. God has called you to attend a celestial board meeting to deliberate with him on matters of destiny.

You can see at once how this raises the whole level of prayer. It is not intended primarily to be centered in my petty needs and woes. To be sure, God is interested in them. They have a place on the agenda. But the agenda itself has been drawn up in heaven and deals with matters of greatest consequence.

John White
Daring to Draw Near

REFLECTING ON YOUR LIFE

Reading the Moment

Reflecting on the Moment

Is there any passage of Scripture that comes to mind that sheds light on this moment?

Responding to the Moment

Reaching up prayerfully

Reaching out personally

And Abraham believed God, and it was reckoned to him as righteousness, and he was called the friend of God. (*James 2:23; see also 2 Chronicles 20:7*)

Then the men rose up from there, and looked down toward Sodom; and Abraham was walking with them to send them off. And the Lord said, "Shall I hide from Abraham what I am about to do?" (*Genesis 18:16-17*)

No longer do I call you slaves, for the slave does not know what his master is doing; but I have called you friends, for all things that I have heard from My Father I have made known to you. (*John 15:15*)

Date

The most holy and necessary practice in our spiritual life is the presence of God. That means finding constant pleasure in His divine company, speaking humbly and lovingly with Him in all seasons, at every moment.

Brother Lawrence
The Practice of the Presence of God

REFLECTING ON YOUR LIFE

Reading the Moment

Reflecting on the Moment

Is there any passage of Scripture that comes to mind that sheds light on this moment?

Responding to the Moment

Reaching up prayerfully

Reaching out personally

The Lord is my shepherd,
I shall not want.
He makes me to lie down in green pastures;
He leads me beside quiet waters.
He restores my soul;
He guides me in the paths of righteousness
For His name's sake.

Even though I walk through the valley of the shadow of death,
I fear no evil; for Thou art with me;
Thy rod and Thy staff, they comfort me.
Thou dost prepare a table before me in the presence of my enemies;
Thou hast anointed my head with oil;
My cup overflows.
Surely goodness and lovingkindness will follow me all the days of my life,
And I will dwell in the house of the Lord forever.

(Psalm 23)

MOMENTS IN THE SCRIPTURES

When I first started growing as a Christian, I thought at least one measurement for a person's love for God was how long and how hard he or she studied the Bible. If you accept that premise, as I consciously or unconsciously did, it seemed logical that the tangible evidence of that love could be seen in the library of books you accumulated to help with those studies.

Consequently, the formative stages of my spiritual growth were marked not by dramatic changes in character or sudden increases in kindness but by an ever-expanding wall of bookshelves. What was growing, of course, was not so much a soul as it was a library that in many ways insulated the soul from all forms of growth except intellectual.

If you follow that logic far enough, as I did, where you end up is seminary, because seminary is where the books are and where the people are who can teach you how to use them. From seminary you graduate in hopes of finding some-place where you can put to use what you have learned in those books. Which invariably means some field of teaching, whether that teaching is in a church or a Bible college or in some other seminary.

Don't get me wrong. Teachers are vital to the body of Christ. Like quarter-backs on a football team, their role cannot be overestimated. My concern is, what besides quarterbacks are we producing? And what besides a skill in those quarterbacks are we nurturing? Is it love? If so, for what? Is it love for the coach—or for the team or the game, for that matter—or is it simply the love of quarterbacking?

Misplaced love.

I think that is the issue we are confronted with when we come to the Scriptures. The issue of our love and where it lies.

Is it the love of words that excites us?

Or is it the love of the One who wrote them?

Is it the love of solving puzzles, albeit biblical ones, that brings us to the Bible?

Or is it the love of Him whose activity—like the path of the wind or how bones form in the womb of a pregnant woman—is beyond understanding?

Is it the love of learning that stimulates our study?

Or is it the love of Him who teaches us?

When our love is properly directed, then and only then is the context accurately established for understanding the words found in the Scriptures.

Which are the very words of God.

Spoken to reveal His love to a wayward world.

Revealed not for information's sake

    but for the sake of wooing us,

        one by one,

            into a deeper and more intimate

                relationship with Him.   43

Date *March 26, 1998*

The Bible was written in tears and to tears it will yield its best treasures. God has nothing to say to the frivolous man.

A.W. Tozer
God Tells the Man Who Cares

REFLECTING ON YOUR LIFE

Reading the Moment

Last night on the evening news and this morning in the newspaper the story was ~~related~~ told of 2 Arkansas boys, age 11 and 13, who set off a fire alarm at their school and ambushed the students and teachers as they emptied the school building. The boys, dressed in ~~camoflage~~ camouflage, used a 30.06 rifle and a .44 caliber rifle with scopes, and in 4 minutes fired some 27 shots. Four school girls and a teacher were killed. Ten others were wounded. Why? The reasons reported in the news coverage varied from gang affiliation to violence in films to easy access to guns to the place of hunting in Southern culture to rejection from girls. What was the reason? How could such a horrible crime come from such young children?

Reflecting on the Moment

I asked myself that question as I put down the newspaper and picked up my Bible. I was reading in Proverbs 1 when this passage leapt off the page like a head line: "Hear, my son, your father's instruction, and do not forsake your mother's teaching. Indeed they are a graceful wreath to your head, and ornaments about your neck. My son, if sinners entice you, do not consent. If they say, 'Come with us, let us lie in wait for blood, let us ambush the innocent without cause'... My son, do not walk in the way with them." As I reflected on that passage and on the questions raised in the news coverage, it seemed to me that though there might have been many factors that played into the violence, the single most determinative factor was the boys' response or lack of response to parental guidance.

Is there any passage of Scripture that comes to mind that sheds light on this moment?

Prov. 3:1-4 Parental teaching adds life and peace to a child's life.
Prov. 4:20-27 Parallel passage, stressing the importance of watching over your heart with all diligence for from it flow the springs of life.

Responding to the Moment

Reaching up prayerfully

Dear God, how can such terrible things come from the hands of such young children? A boy 11 and a boy 13. Cold-blooded killers, Lord. And it no longer seems like an isolated incident. Things like this are beginning to happen all over the country, all over the world. What is happening to our world? What is happening to our country, our neighborhoods, our families? Help us as parents to wake up to our responsibilities in teaching our children a better way than violence.

Reaching out personally

Hearing about this shocking story and reading the passage in Proverbs makes me realize the importance of being involved not only in the lives of my children but in the lives of other children in my community. I have been involved with a ministry to junior high & high school students called Young Life, and today's headlines underscore the importance of ministries like this. I want to be more involved with that ministry, to give more, to pray more, and to volunteer more.

Open my eyes, that I may behold
Wonderful things from Thy law.

My soul is crushed with longing
After Thine ordinances at all times.

My soul weeps because of grief;
Strengthen me according to Thy word.
(Psalm 119:18, 20, 28)

Date

In our meditation we ponder the chosen text on the strength of the promise that it has something utterly personal to say to us for this day and for our Christian life, that it is not only God's Word for the Church, but also God's Word for us individually. We expose ourselves to the specific word until it addresses us personally. And when we do this, we are doing no more than the simplest, untutored Christian does every day; we read God's Word as God's Word for us.

Dietrich Bonhoeffer
Life Together

REFLECTING ON YOUR LIFE

Reading the Moment

Reflecting on the Moment

Is there any passage of Scripture that comes to mind that sheds light on this moment?

Responding to the Moment

Reaching up prayerfully

Reaching out personally

Thy word is a lamp to my feet,
And a light to my path.
(*Psalm 119:105*)

Date

God has provided us with these scriptures that present us with his Word. Loving God means loving both what God speaks to us and the way God speaks to us. It follows that we bring the leisure and attentiveness of lovers to this text. . . . Lovers don't take a quick look, get a "message" or a "meaning" and then run off and gossip with their friends about how they feel. Lovers savor the words, relishing every nuance of what is said and written.

Eugene Peterson

REFLECTING ON YOUR LIFE

Reading the Moment

Reflecting on the Moment

Is there any passage of Scripture that comes to mind that sheds light on this moment?

Responding to the Moment

Reaching up prayerfully

Reaching out personally

And I shall delight in Thy commandments,
Which I love.
And I shall lift up my hands to Thy commandments,
Which I love;
And I will meditate on Thy statutes.

(Psalm 119:47-48)

Date

Reading the scriptures is not as easy as it seems since in our academic world we tend to make anything and everything we read subject to analysis and discussion. But the word of God should lead us first of all to contemplation and meditation. Instead of taking the words apart, we should bring them together in our innermost being; instead of wondering if we agree or disagree, we should wonder which words are directly spoken to us and connect directly with our most personal story. Instead of thinking about the words as potential subjects for an interesting dialogue or paper, we should be willing to let them penetrate into the most hidden corners of our heart, even to those places where no other word has yet found entrance. Then and only then can the word bear fruit as seed sown in rich soil. Only then can we really "hear and understand."

Henri Nouwen
Reaching Out

REFLECTING ON YOUR LIFE

Reading the Moment

Reflecting on the Moment

Is there any passage of Scripture that comes to mind that sheds light on this moment?

Responding to the Moment

Reaching up prayerfully

Reaching out personally

And the one on whom seed was sown on the good soil, this is the man who hears the word and understands it; who indeed bears fruit, and brings forth, some a hundredfold, some sixty, and some thirty. (*Matthew 13:23*)

Date

Whereas the study of Scripture centers on exegesis, the meditation of Scripture centers on internalizing and personalizing the passage. The written Word becomes a living word addressed to you. This is not a time for technical studies, or analysis, or even the gathering of factual material to share with others. Set aside all tendencies toward arrogance and with a humble heart receive the word addressed to you. Often I find kneeling especially appropriate for this particular time.

Richard Foster
Celebration of Discipline

REFLECTING ON YOUR LIFE

Reading the Moment

Reflecting on the Moment

Is there any passage of Scripture that comes to mind that sheds light on this moment?

Responding to the Moment

Reaching up prayerfully

Reaching out personally

Man shall not live by bread alone, but on every word that proceeds out of the mouth of God. (*Matthew 4:4*)

Date

God is here and He is speaking—these truths are back of all other Bible truths; without them there could be no revelation at all. God did not write a book and send it by messenger to be read at a distance by unaided minds. He spoke a Book and lives in His spoken words, constantly speaking His words and causing the power of them to persist across the years.

A.W. Tozer
The Pursuit of God

REFLECTING ON YOUR LIFE

Reading the Moment

Reflecting on the Moment

Is there any passage of Scripture that comes to mind that sheds light on this moment?

Responding to the Moment

Reaching up prayerfully

Reaching out personally

The word of God is living and active and sharper than any two-edged sword, and piercing as far as the division of soul and spirit, of both joints and marrow, and able to judge the thoughts and intentions of the heart. *(Hebrews 4:12)*

MOMENTS AT WORK

It is, I think, hardest to hear God—or anybody else for that matter—in the drone of our daily routine. It seems not to matter much if the gears of that routine grind indoors or outdoors, in an office or a home, in a classroom or a church room.

Each of those places seems to have its own set of clockwork rhythms. Whether set to the minute or the hour or the setting of the sun, each has its own way of ordering our steps and occupying our thoughts.

Which makes it difficult to hear.

Like Martha, maybe we are too distracted by our work to hear.

Like the man who passed up the dinner invitation because he had business to attend to, maybe we are too driven by our work to hear.

Whether it's the drivenness of work or the distractions created by the work, the workplace is often the least conducive place for the wisdom of God to be heard. Yet the voice of wisdom calls from the teeming center of such a place, Solomon says (Proverbs 1:20-21, 8:1-3). From the hustle and bustle of the streets. From the comings and goings at the gates of commerce. From the crowded intersections of life.

And unless we should forget . . .

It was to shepherds at work in their fields that the message from heaven came.

It was to fishermen cleaning their nets that the call to become disciples came.

It was to soldiers on a Friday shift that the word of forgiveness came.

I wonder. How many of the soldiers who showed up for work that day heard that word? Only one that we know of. A centurion. Assigned to the dirty work of overseeing the execution of three common criminals. All day long the centurion went about the routine of his work, waiting for them to die. Watching, as one by one they did. Listening, as they gasped their last words.

As he waited there, what he saw and heard from one of them made him realize that it was no common criminal who died on one of those crosses.

"Truly this man was the Son of God!"

The other soldiers put in their time and were paid their day's wages.

One of them even took home a bonus—a garment he was lucky enough to win.

But only the centurion, only the centurion heard

    what God had spoken

        during that routine workday

            on that Friday afternoon shift.

Date *Sometime in 1990, I think*

In running the church, I seize the initiative. I take charge. I take responsibility for motivation and recruitment, for showing the way, for getting things started. . . .

By contrast, the [care] of souls is a cultivated awareness that God has already seized the initiative. The traditional doctrine defining this truth is prevenience: God everywhere and always seizing the initiative. He gets things going. He had and continues to have the first word. Prevenience is the conviction that God has been working diligently, redemptively, and strategically before I appeared on the scene, before I was aware there was something here to do. . . .

We learn to be attentive to the divine action already in process so that the previously unheard word of God is heard, the previously unattended act of God is noticed.

Running-the-church questions are: What do we do? How can we get things going again?

[Care]-of-souls questions are: What has God been doing here? What traces of grace can I discern in this life? What history of love can I read in this group? What has God set in motion that I can get in on?

Eugene Peterson
The Contemplative Pastor

REFLECTING ON YOUR LIFE

Reading the Moment

I was working at Insight for Living, where I co-authored study guides for Chuck Swindoll's radio ministry. I came to work that day about 7:30 in the morning and went down the hall to get a cup of coffee when I ran into Ken Meeberg there. He had come to work there ~~only~~ only a few months earlier and had been diagnosed with having pancreatic cancer. It appeared terminal. The transmission had just gone out in my car, and when he asked me how I was doing, my frustration with the car came out. Then, in something of a kind and almost fatherly way, he told me: "Be thankful for any problem that writing a check will solve."

Reflecting on the Moment

The words fell into my heart like a proverb that had been distilled from a lifetime of living. The words had authority because Ken's life had authority — the authority of someone who was walking through the valley of the shadow of death with God at his side every step of the way. He had a problem that writing a check couldn't solve. I felt ashamed of myself for allowing something as trivial as a transmission to ruin my day. Here he was, coming to work every day with pancreatic cancer and filling each of those days with thanksgiving and focused on others. There I was, grumbling about a simple mechanical problem, thinking only of myself and how it affected me. "Be thankful for any problem that writing a check will solve." And ever since that morning, because of Ken Meeborg, I have been.

Is there any passage of Scripture that comes to mind that sheds light on this moment?

Do all things without grumbling — Phil. 2:14
In everything give thanks; for this is God's will for you in Christ Jesus.
  1 Thess 5:18

Responding to the Moment

Reaching up prayerfully

Thank you, Lord, for Ken Meeborg, and for the beautiful way he lived and died. He was a good man. I'll never forget him. Though I didn't know him well, what I knew of him profoundly affected me. Help me to never forget the example of his life or the gentle wisdom that came from his lips that morning in the coffee room at work.

Reaching out personally

I want to make a concerted effort at being more thankful and less complaining about my life. I want to live in the awareness that all of life is a gift, that each and every day I wake up is a gift, a new day that has been given me to live and to love and to be loved. Today I'm going to try to express my appreciation to the people around me, starting with Judy and the kids and from there to my mom and some close friends.

Truly, truly, I say to you, the Son can do nothing of Himself, unless it is something He sees the Father doing; for whatever the Father does, these things the Son also does in like manner. . . . I can do nothing on my own initiative. (*John 5:19, 30a*)

Date

In a parish church in England stands a monument to Henry Hoare, who designed and made the landscape garden of Stourhead. Inscribed on the monument are the words:

In memory of Henry Hoare Esq.

Who died Sept. 8th 1785, aged 80 years.

Under the inscription is a scroll on which are these words:

Ye who have viewed in Pleasure's choicest hour
The earth embellished on these banks of Stour,
With grateful Reverence to this Marble lean,
Rais'd to the Friendly Founder of the Scene.
Here, with pure love of smiling Nature warm'd,
This far-fam'd Demy-Paradise he form'd:
And happier still, here learn'd from Heaven to find
A sweeter Eden in a Bounteous Mind.
Thankful these fair & flowery paths he trod,
And priz'd them only as they led to GOD.

The English Garden

REFLECTING ON YOUR LIFE

Reading the Moment

Reflecting on the Moment

Is there any passage of Scripture that comes to mind that sheds light on this moment?

Responding to the Moment

Reaching up prayerfully

Reaching out personally

Then the Lord God formed man of dust from the ground, and breathed into his nostrils the breath of life; and man became a living being. And the Lord God planted a garden toward the east, in Eden; and there He placed the man whom He had formed. And out of the ground the Lord God caused to grow every tree that is pleasing to the sight and good for food; the tree of life also in the midst of the garden, and the tree of the knowledge of good and evil. . . .

Then the Lord God took the man and put him into the garden of Eden to cultivate it and keep it. And the Lord God commanded the man, saying, "From any tree of the garden you may eat freely; but from the tree of the knowledge of good and evil you shall not eat, for in the day that you eat from it you shall surely die." (*Genesis 2:7-9, 15-17*)

Date

Since we began our work, something wonderful is happening. More and more poor people are coming from the villages into Calcutta, but there is a difference. Ordinary people are beginning to get concerned. Before, they used to pass by a person dying on the streets, but now, when they see something like that, they immediately do something. . . .

I did not know that our work would grow so fast or go so far. I never doubted that it would live, but I did not think it would be like this. Doubt I never had, because I had this conviction that if God blesses it, it will prosper. Humanly speaking, it is impossible, out of the question. Because none of us has got the experience. None of us has got the things that the world looks for. This is the miracle of all those little Sisters all around the world. God is using them—they are just little instruments in His hands. But they all have their conviction. As long as any of us has this conviction we are all right. The work will prosper. But the moment we begin to say, "It is I, it is my work," then it becomes selfish. Nothing will be necessary. The Congregation and the work will die.

Mother Teresa

Mother Teresa by Desmond Doig

REFLECTING ON YOUR LIFE

Reading the Moment

Reflecting on the Moment

Is there any passage of Scripture that comes to mind that sheds light on this moment?

Responding to the Moment

Reaching up prayerfully

Reaching out personally

Beware lest you forget the Lord your God by not keeping His commandments and His ordinances and His statutes which I am commanding you today; lest, when you have eaten and are satisfied, and have built good houses and lived in them, and when your herds and your flocks multiply, and your silver and gold multiply, and all that you have multiplies, then your heart becomes proud, and you forget the Lord your God who brought you out from the land of Egypt, out of the house of slavery. He led you through the great and terrible wilderness, with its fiery serpents and scorpions and thirsty ground where there was no water; He brought water for you out of the rock of flint. In the wilderness He fed you manna which your fathers did not know, that He might humble you and that He might test you, to do good for you in the end. Otherwise, you may say in your heart, "My power and the strength of my hand made me this wealth." But you shall remember the Lord your God, for it is He who is giving you power to make wealth, that He may confirm His covenant which He swore to your fathers, as it is this day. And it shall come about if you ever forget the Lord your God, and go after other gods and serve them and worship them, I testify against you today that you shall surely perish. Like the nations that the Lord makes to perish before you, so you shall perish; because you would not listen to the voice of the Lord your God. (*Deuteronomy 8:11-20*)

Date

We ought not to be weary of doing little things for the love of God, who regards not the greatness of the work, but the love with which it is performed.

Brother Lawrence
The Practice of the Presence of God

REFLECTING ON YOUR LIFE

Reading the Moment

Reflecting on the Moment

Is there any passage of Scripture that comes to mind that sheds light on this moment?

Responding to the Moment

Reaching up prayerfully

Reaching out personally

If I speak with the tongues of men and of angels, but do not have love, I have become a noisy gong or a clanging cymbal. And if I have the gift of prophecy, and know all mysteries and all knowledge; and if I have all faith, so as to remove mountains, but do not have love, I am nothing. And if I give all my possessions to feed the poor, and if I deliver my body to be burned, but do not have love, it profits me nothing. (*1 Corinthians 13:1-3*)

Date

In the beginning of his novitiate [Brother Lawrence] spent the hours appointed for private prayer in thinking of God, so as to convince his mind of, and to impress deeply upon
his heart, the divine existence, rather by devout sentiments, and submission to the lights
of faith, than by studied reasonings and elaborate meditations. That by this short and sure
method he exercised himself in the knowledge and love of God, resolving to use his
utmost endeavor to live in a continual sense of His presence, and, if possible never to forget Him more.

That when he had thus in prayer filled his mind with great sentiments of that infinite Being, he went to his work appointed in the kitchen (for he was cook to the society). There having first considered severally the things his office required, and when and
how each thing was to be done, he spent all the intervals of his time, as well before as
after his work, in prayer.

That when he began his business, he said to God, with a filial trust in Him: O my
God, since Thou art with me, and I must now, in obedience to Thy commands, apply
my mind to these outward things, I beseech Thee to grant me the grace to continue in
Thy presence; and to this end do Thou prosper me with Thy assistance, receive all my
works, and possess all my affections.

As he proceeded in his work he continued his familiar conversation with his Maker,
imploring His grace, and offering to Him all his actions.

When he had finished he examined himself how he had discharged his duty; if he
found well, he returned thanks to God; if otherwise, he asked pardon, and, without being
discouraged, he set his mind right again, and continued his exercise of the presence of
God as if he had never deviated from it. "Thus," said he, "by rising after my falls, and by
frequently renewed acts of faith and love, I am come to a state wherein it would be difficult for me not to think of God as it was at first to accustom myself to it." . . .

His very countenance was edifying, such a sweet and calm devotion appearing in it
as could not but affect the beholders. And it was observed that in the greatest hurry of
business in the kitchen he still preserved his recollection and heavenly-mindedness. He
was never hasty nor loitering, but did each thing in its season, with an even, uninter-
rupted composure and tranquillity of spirit. "The time of business," said he, "does not
with me differ from the time of prayer; and in the noise and clatter of my kitchen, while
several persons are at the same time calling for different things, I possess God in as great
tranquillity as if I were upon my knees at the blessed sacrament."

Introductory remarks from
The Practice of the Presence of God
by Brother Lawrence

REFLECTING ON YOUR LIFE

Reading the Moment

Reflecting on the Moment

Is there any passage of Scripture that comes to mind that sheds light on this moment?

Responding to the Moment

Reaching up prayerfully

Reaching out personally

Whatever you do, do your work heartily, as for the Lord rather than for men; knowing that from the Lord you will receive the reward of the inheritance. It is the Lord Christ whom you serve. (*Colossians 3:23-24*)

Date

If the job is decent and useful, there really is no dirty job.

I can scrub floors, in my home or at an office; I can cope with garbage—at my sink or on a truck. I may not like to do it, but I will thank God I have the strength to do it. I will not consider myself too good to do it. I will not ask anyone else to do something I wouldn't do myself.

And I will discover rewards I might otherwise have missed.

Our son, the night when after much nagging he'd carried out the trash. (I'd done it all week.) "Mom, go look at the sky, it's unbelievable!" he exclaimed. Then, grinning, "Just think—I wouldn't have seen the sunset if I hadn't carried out the trash!"

Al Matthews, our rector—the day I surprised him in shirt sleeves at the church, a large can of refuse on his shoulder. His unassuming comment: "Oh, I always do this, I like to, it's one way of giving me humility; it reminds me I'm no better than anybody else."

And the inevitable comparison came: the night of the Last Supper. Jesus kneeling to wash his disciples' dirty feet. And how Peter protested, "Don't do that, Lord—oh, no, not you!" And Jesus' reply that we all must be equal, there is no high nor low in the Kingdom of God.

Remembering that, I can find God in the lowliest job I must do. I can wash a baby's diapers, empty a bedpan, cleanse a festering sore. I can gladly soil my hands and bow my back because God is in my heart, reminding me of the marvel of life in all its aspects, and the miracle of my own humanity.

Marjorie Holmes
How Can I Find You, God?

REFLECTING ON YOUR LIFE

Reading the Moment

Reflecting on the Moment

Is there any passage of Scripture that comes to mind that sheds light on this moment?

Responding to the Moment

Reaching up prayerfully

Reaching out personally

And so when He had washed their feet, and taken His garments, and reclined at the table again, He said to them, "Do you know what I have done to you? You call me Teacher and Lord; and you are right, for so I am. If I then, the Lord and the Teacher, washed your feet, you also ought to wash another's feet. For I gave you an example that you also should do as I did to you. Truly, truly, I say to you, a slave is not greater than his master; neither is one who is sent greater than the one who sent him." *(John 13:12-16)*

MOMENTS WITH OTHERS

More often than not, the words God speaks are mediated words, coming to us not only in a variety of ways but through a variety of people. Take Jesus and His cousin John the Baptist, for example. They couldn't be closer in terms of their message. But in terms of how that message came packaged, they couldn't be further apart.

Noting this contrast to an unresponsive crowd, Jesus said, "We played the flute for you, and you did not dance; we sang a dirge, and you did not mourn. For John came neither eating nor drinking, and they say, 'He has a demon!' The Son of Man came eating and drinking, and they say, 'Behold, a gluttonous man and a drunkard, a friend of tax-gatherers and sinners!'" (Matthew 11:17-19)

If we have serious issues with asceticism, we might never have seen past the camel skins that John the Baptist wore or the diet of locusts and honey that he ate. If we get turned off with people who pass judgment, we might never have heard anything past the prophet's first finger-wagging word, "Repent!"

If, on the other hand, we have trouble with people who enjoy a little more religious liberty than we think they should, we might never have seen past the people Jesus associated with or the parties He attended. If we are set in our ways, we might have missed Him who Himself is the way, the truth, and the life.

To be sure, God has spoken through prophets (Hebrews 1:1).

But He has also spoken through preschoolers (Matthew 21:15-16).

And through everyone in between (Acts 2:1-18).

Knowing that makes a difference how we listen. And to whom we listen. If we think God only speaks through religious representatives, whether they be pastors or teachers or evangelists, we will likely be skeptical of the other voices through which God is speaking (Acts 2:13), or worse, we may even become indignant to those voices (Matthew 21:15).

Either way, if we're not careful, we will miss what God is saying.

"He who has ears to hear, let him hear," Jesus said, and He said it as a warning, because though we all have ears, so many things keep us from hearing, not the least of which is our attitude toward others, an attitude of skepticism and indignance.

As you go through the next week, go through it listening, *really* listening. To everyone around you. And to everything they say, verbal and nonverbal. Try not to judge what you hear too quickly. Wait. Watch. Listen. And maybe you will discover the thrill of God speaking to you in some way through the life of another person.

Date *April 23, 1987*

He comes to us in such a way that we can always turn him down. . . . God comes to us in the hungry man we do not have to feed, comes to us in the lonely man we do not have to comfort, comes to us in all the desperate human need of people everywhere that we are always free to turn our backs upon.

Frederick Buechner
The Hungering Dark

REFLECTING ON YOUR LIFE

Reading the Moment

I was working at Insight for Living and my supervisor, Bob Ludwig, had arranged a meeting with his friend, Vernon Grounds, who was in town. Vernon was in his 70s and president emeritus of Denver Conservative Baptist Seminary. He was as well-read and as sharp-minded and as keen-witted as any younger scholar at the top of his form. He was a gracious man. Congenial. ~~Unpretentious~~. Unpretentious. A good listener. And humble. After two unselfish hours of questions and answers and conversation, the time we had with him drew to a close. I extended my hand to him, and instead of shaking it, he hugged me in a warm and genuine embrace, and he said a blessing for me. And at that moment, more than any, touched me deeply.

Reflecting on the Moment

For the two hours I was with Vernon Grounds, I felt in the presence of Christ. I saw the kindness of Christ in his eyes, heard the tenderness of Christ in his voice, felt the love of Christ in his embrace. I extended my hand. He extended himself. He hugged me and blessed me and left me with a fragrant aroma of Christ that has stayed with me to this day.

Is there any passage of Scripture that comes to mind that sheds light on this moment?

That we are "a fragrant aroma of Christ" to those around us.

Responding to the Moment

Reaching up prayerfully

Dear God, thank you for that brief encounter with Vernon Grounds, and for what I saw of your Son in his life. Help me to so live my life, Lord, that during the time I spend with others, they might see something of Jesus in me. Forgive me for all of the times I have gotten in the way and obscured the view.

Reaching out personally

I want to remember how good I felt when Vernon Grounds left that day so I can remember to pass on to others what he passed on to me — a fragrant aroma of Christ. Especially I want my children to feel that way after they've been with me. I know that my teasing gets in the way of them seeing Christ in me, I know am going to really try to hug them more and speak the words that will be a blessing to their lives.

Now there was a certain rich man, and he habitually dressed in purple and fine linen, gaily living in splendor every day. And a certain poor man named Lazarus was laid at his gate, covered with sores, and longing to be fed with the crumbs which were falling from the rich man's table; besides, even the dogs were coming and licking his sores. Now it came about that the poor man died and he was carried away by the angels to Abraham's bosom; and the rich man also died and was buried. And in Hades he lifted up his eyes, being in torment, and saw Abraham far away, and Lazarus in his bosom. And he cried out and said, "Father Abraham, have mercy on me, and send Lazarus, that he may dip the tip of his finger in water and cool off my tongue, for I am in agony in this flame."

But Abraham said, "Child, remember that during your life you received your good things, and likewise Lazarus bad things; but now he is being comforted here, and you are in agony. And besides all this, between us and you there is a great chasm fixed, in order that those who wish to come over from here to you may not be able, and that none may cross over from there to us." (*Luke 16:19-26*)

Date

It is a serious thing to live in a society of possible gods and goddesses, to remember that the dullest and most uninteresting person you talk to may one day become a creature which, if you saw it now, you would be strongly tempted to worship, or else a horror and a corruption such as you now meet, if at all, only in a nightmare. . . . You have never talked to a mere mortal. Nations, cultures, arts, civilization—these are mortal, and their life is to ours as the life of a gnat. But it is immortals whom we joke with, work with, marry, snub, and exploit—immortal horrors or everlasting splendours. This does not mean that we are to be perpetually solemn. We must play. But our merriment must be of that kind (and it is, in fact, the merriest kind) which exists between people who have, from the outset, taken each other seriously—no flippancy, no superiority, no presumption. And our charity must be real and costly love, with deep feeling for the sins in spite of which we love the sinner—no mere tolerance or indulgence which parodies love as flippancy parodies merriment. Next to the Blessed Sacrament itself, your neighbour is the holiest object presented to your senses.

C.S. Lewis
The Weight of Glory

REFLECTING ON YOUR LIFE

Reading the Moment

Reflecting on the Moment

Is there any passage of Scripture that comes to mind that sheds light on this moment?

Responding to the Moment

Reaching up prayerfully

Reaching out personally

Therefore we do not lose heart, but though our outer man is decaying, yet our inner man is being renewed day by day. For momentary, light affliction is producing for us an eternal weight of glory far beyond all comparison, while we look not at the things which are seen, but at the things which are not seen; for the things which are seen are temporal, but the things which are not seen are eternal. (*2 Corinthians 4:16-18*)

Date

A girl came from outside India to join the Missionaries of Charity. We have a rule that the very next day the new arrivals must go to the Home for the Dying. So I told this girl: "You saw Father during Holy Mass, with what love and care he touched Jesus in the Host. Do the same when you go to the Home for the Dying, because it is the same Jesus you will find there in the broken bodies of the poor." And they went. After three hours the newcomer came back and said to me with a big smile—I have never seen a smile quite like that—"Mother, I have been touching the body of Christ for three hours." And I said to her: "How—what did you do?" She replied: "When we arrived there, they brought a man who had fallen into a drain, and been there for some time. He was covered with wounds and dirt and maggots, and I cleaned him and I knew I was touching the body of Christ."

Mother Teresa
A Gift for God

REFLECTING ON YOUR LIFE

Reading the Moment

Reflecting on the Moment

Is there any passage of Scripture that comes to mind that sheds light on this moment?

Responding to the Moment

Reaching up prayerfully

Reaching out personally

Then the King will say to those on His right, "Come, you who are blessed of My Father, inherit the kingdom prepared for you from the foundation of the world. For I was hungry, and you gave Me something to eat; I was thirsty, and you gave Me drink; I was a stranger, and you invited Me in; naked, and you clothed Me; I was sick, and you visited Me; I was in prison, and you came to Me."

Then the righteous will answer Him, saying, "Lord, when did we see You hungry, and feed You, or thirsty, and give You drink? And when did we see You a stranger, and invite You in, or naked, and clothe You? And when did we see You sick, or in prison, and come to You?"

And the King will answer and say to them, "Truly I say to you, to the extent that you did it to one of these brothers of Mine, even to the least of them, you did it to Me." *(Matthew 25:34-40)*

Date

Old and New Testament stories not only show how serious our obligation is to welcome the stranger into our home, but they also tell us that guests are carrying precious gifts with them, which they are eager to reveal to a receptive host. When Abraham received three strangers at Mamre and offered them water, bread and a fine tender calf, they revealed themselves to him as the Lord announcing that Sarah his wife should give birth to a son (Genesis 18:1-15). When the widow of Zarephath offered food and shelter to Elijah, he revealed himself as a man of God offering her an abundance of oil and meal and raising her son from the dead (1 Kings 17:9-24). When the two travelers to Emmaus invited the stranger, who had joined them on the road to stay with them for the night, he made himself known in the breaking of the bread as their Lord and Saviour (Luke 24:13-35).

When hostility is converted to hospitality then fearful strangers can become guests revealing to their hosts the promise they are carrying with them. Then, in fact, the distinction between host and guest proves to be artificial and evaporates in the recognition of the new found unity.

Thus the biblical stories help us to realize not just that hospitality is an important virtue, but even more that in the context of hospitality guest and host can reveal their most precious gifts and bring new life to each other.

Henri Nouwen

Reaching Out

REFLECTING ON YOUR LIFE

Reading the Moment

Reflecting on the Moment

Is there any passage of Scripture that comes to mind that sheds light on this moment?

Responding to the Moment

Reaching up prayerfully

Reaching out personally

Do not neglect to show hospitality to strangers, for by this some have entertained angels without knowing it. (*Hebrews 13:2*)

Date

It may sound strange to speak of the relationship between parents and children in terms of hospitality. But it belongs to the center of the Christian message that children are not properties to own and rule over, but gifts to cherish and care for. Our children are our most important guests, who enter into our home, ask for careful attention, stay for a while and then leave to follow their own way. . . .

What parents can offer is a home, a place that is receptive but also has the safe boundaries within which their children can develop and discover what is helpful and what is harmful. There their children can ask questions without fear and can experiment with life without the risk of rejection. There they can be encouraged to listen to their own inner selves and to develop the freedom that gives them the courage to leave home and travel on. The hospitable home indeed is the place where father, mother and children can reveal their talents to each other, become present to each other as members of the same human family and support each other in their common struggles.

Henri Nouwen
Reaching Out

REFLECTING ON YOUR LIFE

Reading the Moment

Reflecting on the Moment

Is there any passage of Scripture that comes to mind that sheds light on this moment?

Responding to the Moment

Reaching up prayerfully

Reaching out personally

Behold, children are a gift of the Lord. (*Psalm 127:3a*)

Date

A good relationship has a pattern like a dance and is built on some of the same rules. The partners do not need to hold on tightly, because they move confidently in the same pattern, intricate but gay and swift and free, like a country dance of Mozart's. To touch heavily would be to arrest the pattern and freeze the movement, to check the endlessly changing beauty of its unfolding. There is no heavy hand, only the barest touch in passing. Now arm in arm, now face to face, now back to back—it does not matter which. Because they know they are partners moving to the same rhythm, creating a pattern together, and being invisibly nourished by it.

Anne Morrow Lindbergh
Gift from the Sea

REFLECTING ON YOUR LIFE

Reading the Moment

Reflecting on the Moment

Is there any passage of Scripture that comes to mind that sheds light on this moment?

Responding to the Moment

Reaching up prayerfully

Reaching out personally

I exhort the elders among you, as your fellow elder and witness of the sufferings of Christ, and a partaker also of the glory that is to be revealed, shepherd the flock of God among you, exercising oversight not under compulsion, but voluntarily, according to the will of God; and not for sordid gain, but with eagerness; nor yet as lording it over those allotted to your charge, but proving to be examples to the flock. And when the Chief Shepherd appears, you will receive the unfading crown of glory.

You younger men, likewise, be subject to your elders; and all of you, clothe yourselves with humility toward one another, for God is opposed to the proud, but gives grace to the humble. (*1 Peter 5:1-5*)

MOMENTS IN NATURE

Nature is a grand, sweeping mural that reveals not only the handiwork of its Maker (Psalm 8) but something of who He is (Romans 1:20) and how He works (Proverbs 8:22-31).

When God answered Job out of a whirlwind, all the object lessons He used were drawn from nature (Job 38-41). When Jesus taught, He drew largely from the natural world (Matthew 7:15-23). So did Paul (Galatians 5:22-23) and James (James 1:6, 10-11).

84

The scriptural view of nature is that nature is replete with wisdom and those who want to be wise search for it as if mining for gold and precious stones. Here is a sampling from both Old and New Testaments of what others have found buried there:

For lack of wood the fire goes out,
And where there is no whisperer, contention quiets down. (Proverbs 26:20)

Sow your seed in the morning, and do not be idle in the evening,
for you do not know whether morning or evening sowing will succeed,
or whether both of them alike will be good. (Ecclesiastes 11:6)

I am the true vine, and My Father is the vinedresser. Every branch in Me that does not bear fruit, He takes away; and every branch that bears fruit, He prunes it, that it may bear more fruit. (John 15:1-2)

I planted, Apollos watered, but God was causing the growth. So then neither the one who plants nor the one who waters is anything, but God who causes the growth. (1 Corinthians 3:6-7)

Be patient, therefore, brethren, until the coming of the Lord. Behold, the farmer waits for the precious produce of the soil, being patient about it, until he gets the early and late rains. You too be patient; strengthen your hearts, for the coming of the Lord is at hand. (James 5:7-8)

If you can, take a side road somewhere off the beaten track and spend some time observing some of God's art in the gallery of nature. Once there, begin asking it questions. What does the place tell you about the Artist? What does it reveal about what He values? What does it say about how He works?

What you see there and hear there may whisper to you as subtly as a change of seasons, or it may startle you as suddenly as a clap of thunder. But unless you're there watching, you won't see. And unless you're there listening, you won't hear.

Date   *A Fall day, 1997*

Everybody needs beauty as well as bread, places to play in and pray in, where Nature may heal and cheer and give strength to body and soul.

Only spread a fern-frond over a man's head, and worldly cares are cast out, and freedom and beauty and peace come in.

John Muir
John Muir in His Own Words
compiled by Peter Browning

REFLECTING ON YOUR LIFE

Reading the Moment

I saw a topographical map of Colorado in a bookstore, the western half of it was mountainous, the eastern half was flat. We live not too far from Interstate 25, the highway that separates the mountains in Colorado from the flatland. The contrast between the two parts of the state is striking. The eastern part of the state is monotonous. The western part is majestic. And it is that striking contrast which caught my attention.

Reflecting on the Moment

I started thinking about the mountains and the flatlands, and realized that at one time on earth the most terrifying place to be would have been Western Colorado where a catastrophic geological upheaval occurred. If I were there then, I would have wanted to be in the peaceful eastern part of the state, not in the western part. But today, people don't come to the eastern part of the state for their vacation. They come to the western part. The places of upheaval, in our lives – sometimes catastrophic upheaval – are the very places that God, in His grace, makes beautiful. He takes the tragic and makes something majestic out of it. By the relentless, weathering grace of God, He gives us something beautiful to share with the world.

Is there any passage of Scripture that comes to mind that sheds light on this moment?

He makes everything beautiful in its time — Ecclesiastes 3:11

Responding to the Moment

Reaching up prayerfully

Thank you, God, for the moments of upheaval in my life. I thank you not for the moments themselves but for what you did with the moments over time in my life. Thank you for the new things I have seen and felt because of them. Thank you for the clearer vision you have given me as a result of those upheavals, for ~~this~~ a heart that is more tender & understanding, for a life that is more real, and for something I have to share with others because of those painful times.

Reaching out personally

I tend to be ~~to~~ more of a private person and that is not always good. In keeping my pain private, I am putting a wall up that obscures the view of how God's grace is working in my life. I have some letters to write this weekend to strangers who may have a somewhat idealized impression of who I am and what my life is like. The best that I can I am going to try to let them see some of the things I struggle with so they can see that this is the process God uses in our lives — the process of making all things beautiful in their time.

He makes me lie down in green pastures;
He leads me beside quiet waters.
He restores my soul.

(Psalm 23:2-3a)

Date

The moral law lies at the center of nature and radiates to the circumference. It is the pith and marrow of every substance, every relation, and every process. All things with which we deal, preach to us. What is a farm but a mute gospel? The chaff and the wheat, weeds and plants, blight, rain, insects, sun—it is a sacred emblem from the first furrow of spring to the last stack which the snow of winter overtakes in the fields.

Ralph Waldo Emerson

REFLECTING ON YOUR LIFE

Reading the Moment

Reflecting on the Moment

Is there any passage of Scripture that comes to mind that sheds light on this moment?

Responding to the Moment

Reaching up prayerfully

Reaching out personally

That which you sow does not come to life unless it dies; and that which you sow, you do not sow the body which is to be, but a bare grain, perhaps of wheat or something else. . . . So also is the resurrection from the dead. It is sown a perishable body, it is raised an imperishable body; it is sown in dishonor, it is raised in glory; it is sown in weakness, it is raised in power; it is sown a natural body, it is raised a spiritual body. If there is a natural body, there is also a spiritual body. (*1 Corinthians 15:36-37, 42-44*)

Date

We seem to imagine that since Herod beheaded John the Baptist there is no longer any voice crying in the Wilderness. But no one in the wilderness can possibly make such a mistake. No wilderness in the world is so desolate as to be without God's ministers. The love of God covers all the earth as the sky covers it and fills every pore. And this love has voices heard by all who have ears to hear.

John Muir
John Muir: Life and Work
edited by Sally M. Miller

REFLECTING ON YOUR LIFE

Reading the Moment

Reflecting on the Moment

Is there any passage of Scripture that comes to mind that sheds light on this moment?

Responding to the Moment

Reaching up prayerfully

Reaching out personally

The heavens are telling of the glory of God;
And their expanse is declaring the work of His hands.
Day to day pours forth speech,
And night to night reveals knowledge.
There is no speech, nor are there words;
Their voice is not heard.
Their line has gone out through all the earth,
And their utterances to the end of the world.

(Psalm 19:1-4)

Date

Seeing starts with respect. Respect doesn't come from the depth of our understanding of another individual, or organism, or ecosystem, or nature as a whole. In every instance the scope of our ignorance vastly overshadows that of our knowledge. Respect comes from a belief that the great abyss of our ignorance, a void articulated by the sketchy understanding we possess, contains meaning worthy of our attention and effort, no matter how difficult the task appears. . . .

Seeing nature is a process, partly, of replacing our arrogance with humility. When we respect the reality which fills the abyss of our ignorance, we begin to see.

Steven J. Meyers
On Seeing Nature

REFLECTING ON YOUR LIFE

Reading the Moment

Reflecting on the Moment

Is there any passage of Scripture that comes to mind that sheds light on this moment?

Responding to the Moment

Reaching up prayerfully

Reaching out personally

Four things are small on the earth,
But they are exceedingly wise:
The ants are not a strong folk,
But they prepare their food in the summer;
The badgers are not mighty folk,
Yet they make their houses in the rocks;
The locusts have no king,
Yet all of them go out in ranks;
The lizard you may grasp with the hands,
Yet it is in kings' palaces.

(Proverbs 30:24-28)

Date

God does not come to us by way of syllogism, by a series of abstractions, by a thinking that proceeds from concept to concept, but by way of insights. The ultimate insight is the outcome of *moments* when we are stirred beyond words, of instants of wonder, awe, praise, fear, trembling and radical amazement; of awareness of grandeur, of perceptions we can grasp but are unable to convey, of discoveries of the unknown, of moments in which we abandon the pretense of being acquainted with the world, of *knowledge by acquaintance.* It is at the climax of such moments that we attain the certainty that life has meaning, that time is more than evanescence, that beyond all being there is someone who cares.

Abraham Heschel
God in Search of Man: A Philosophy of Judaism

REFLECTING ON YOUR LIFE

Reading the Moment

Reflecting on the Moment

Is there any passage of Scripture that comes to mind that sheds light on this moment?

Responding to the Moment

Reaching up prayerfully

Reaching out personally

When I consider Thy heavens, the work of Thy fingers,
The moon and the stars, which Thou hast ordained;
What is man, that Thou dost take thought of him?
And the son of man, that Thou dost care for him?
Yet Thou hast made him a little lower than God,
And dost crown him with glory and majesty!

(Psalm 8:3-5)

Date

If you hold to Nature, to the simplicity that is in her, to the small detail that scarcely one man sees, which can so unexpectedly grow into something great and boundless; if you have this love for insignificant things and seek, simply as one who serves, to win the confidence of what seems to be poor: then everything will become easier for you.

Rainer Maria Rilke
Letters to a Young Poet

REFLECTING ON YOUR LIFE

Reading the Moment

Reflecting on the Moment

Is there any passage of Scripture that comes to mind that sheds light on this moment?

Responding to the Moment

Reaching up prayerfully

Reaching out personally

For this reason I say to you, do not be anxious for your life, as to what you shall eat, or what you shall drink; not for your body, as to what you shall put on. Is not life more than food, and the body than clothing? Look at the birds of the air, that they do not sow, neither do they reap, nor gather into barns, and yet your heavenly Father feeds them. Are you not worth much more than they? And which of you by being anxious can add a single cubit to his life's span? And why are you anxious about clothing? Observe how the lilies of the field grow; they do not toil nor do they spin, yet I say to you that even Solomon in all his glory did not clothe himself like one of these. But if God so arrays the grass of the field, which is alive today and tomorrow is thrown into the furnace, will He not much more do so for you, O men of little faith? (*Matthew 6:25-30*)

SECTION SEVEN

MOMENTS OF AWE

Abraham J. Heschel was an extraordinary thinker who taught at the Jewish Theological Seminary of America. He died in 1972. More than any person I have ever read, he captured in his writings what I believe is the true heart of Old Testament faith. Two of my favorite books by him are *Man Is Not Alone: A Philosophy of Religion* and *God in Search of Man: A Philosophy of Judaism.* Every page of these books throbs with life and truth, faith and goodness, beauty and wisdom.

I was an Old Testament major in seminary, but I don't think I ever connected with the heart of the Old Testament until I read Heschel. Within his writings I found something remarkably similar to what I had read in the writings of C.S. Lewis, A.W. Tozer, and many of the great saints of the church.

That something was what each of them said about awe.

Awe is an old word and one that has all but vanished from circulation, at least in its original sense. It is a biblical word for a profoundly spiritual experience. For many of us, it was a moment of awe that brought us to our knees, revealing to us maybe for the first time who Jesus was and what He was asking of us, which was nothing less than our lives.

In *Man Is Not Alone*, Heschel describes such a moment. "In every man's life there are moments when there is a lifting of the veil at the horizon of the known, opening a sight of the eternal. Each of us has at least once in his life experienced the momentous reality of God. Each of us has once caught a glimpse of the beauty, peace and power that flow through the souls devoted to Him. But such experiences or inspirations are rare events. To some people they are like shooting stars, passing unremembered. In others they kindle a light that is never quenched."

In *God in Search of Man*, he adds: "The loss of awe is the great block to insight. A return to reverence is the first prerequisite for a revival of wisdom, for the discovery of the world as an allusion to God. Wisdom comes from awe

98

rather than from shrewdness. It is evoked not in moments of calculation but in moments of being in rapport with the mystery of reality. The greatest insights happen in moments of awe."

Moments of awe are moments when we are the most vulnerable to grace.

Without those moments, we are vulnerable to everything else.

C.S. Lewis called such moments "'patches of Godlight' in the woods of our experience."

In this section of the journal, think of the times when you experienced such moments in your own life. Maybe it was the moment you came to faith. Or maybe it was the moment that kept you from walking away from your faith. Maybe it wasn't a Damascus Road experience or even an Emmaus Road experience. But it was *your* experience. And it happened on the road *you* were traveling.

For a moment on that road the clouds between heaven and earth parted. Remember that moment forever. For that patch of Godlight, however brief or far back in your past, may be the very light that leads you to safety when someday the woods grow dark and the way out of the darkness seems impossible.

Date *A church conference in 1988*

Every one of us has had experiences which we have not been able to explain—a sudden sense of loneliness, or a feeling of wonder or awe in the face of the universal vastness. Or we have had a fleeting visitation of light like an illumination from some other sun, giving us in a quick flash an assurance that we are from another world, that our origins are divine. . . . Explain such things as we will, I think we have not been fair to the facts until we allow at least the possibility that such experiences may arise from the presence of God in the world and His persistent effort to communicate with mankind.

A.W. Tozer
The Pursuit of God

REFLECTING ON YOUR LIFE

Reading the Moment

I was at a church conference with probably 2,000 to 2,500 other people, and we were all singing the song, "Holy and Anointed One." During the chorus are the words "Jesus, I love you," and as we sang, a moment of awe came over me. Tears streamed down my face, and I sang louder with every stanza. I felt such love for Jesus that I didn't want the song to end. I've never had a moment like that when I was singing, and I've never had one since, ~~although I tried~~ in spite of my efforts to try to recreate the moment by singing that same song and trying to infuse it with the same emotions.

Reflecting on the Moment

In much of my ~~chu~~ church experience, singing was something you had to go through to get to the good stuff in the service, which was the sermon, which wasn't always good but at least always held out the hope that something good might be heard there. Whenever I thought about singing in Heaven, I associated it with the singing I had been used to. All that changed that day at the conference. I was given, I think, in that moment a taste of what Heaven was like. I was allowed a fleeting visitation like an illumination from another sun, a quick flash that revealed to me some of the joy and *ecstasy* that awaited me in Heaven. I can't explain the moment in words. But I will never forget it. And I will never forget the longing it created in me to be there with Christ.

Is there any passage of Scripture that comes to mind that sheds light on this moment?

Eye has not seen or he ear heard what all God has prepared for the hearts of those that love Him. (Somewhere in 1st or 2nd Corinthians)

Responding to the Moment

Reaching up prayerfully

Jesus, I <u>do</u> love you. Please help me to love you more. I pray for more moments like the one I had that day singing to you, moments that turn my eyes and my heart and my dreams onto you. You promised to disclose yourself to those who loved you and kept your commandments. Help me to love you more and to be more obedient to you so I could be given more of those moments of disclosure.

Reaching out personally

What can I do on my part to love Jesus more and to be more obey Him more? If I realized more just how much He loved me, I think I would naturally be drawn to love Him more. How do I do that? Searching the Scriptures with a view to seeing His love. Studying my life to see how He has extended His love through the people in my life & the circumstances in my life. Is there any area in my life that isn't in obedience to Him? That's what I'm going to think about today and pray about.

There came therefore a voice out of heaven: "I have both glorified it [My name], and will glorify it again." The multitude therefore, who stood by and heard it, were saying that it had thundered; others were saying, "An angel has spoken to Him." Jesus answered and said, "This voice has not come for My sake, but for your sakes." *(John 12:28-30)*

Date

Singer John Michael Talbot was once part of a folk-rock group that performed with the Grateful Dead, Jefferson Airplane, and Janis Joplin. During his band's 1971 tour, he was alone at a Holiday Inn when a brilliant light filled his room. In the midst of the light stood Jesus in radiant robes, "his arms outstretched in a combination of gentleness and strength," as Talbot described the awe-inspiring moment. That moment, understandably, changed the entire course of his life. Now a lay Franciscan monk, Talbot uses his music in a reflective way to sing of the loveliness of the Jesus he once saw at that Holiday Inn.

John Michael Talbot

Story told to the *Colorado Springs Gazette Telegraph*

REFLECTING ON YOUR LIFE

Reading the Moment

Reflecting on the Moment

Is there any passage of Scripture that comes to mind that sheds light on this moment?

Responding to the Moment

Reaching up prayerfully

Reaching out personally

Now Saul, still breathing threats and murder against the disciples of the Lord, went to the high priest, and asked for letters from him to the synagogues at Damascus, so that if he found any belonging to the Way, both men and women, he might bring them bound to Jerusalem. And it came about that as he journeyed, he was approaching Damascus, and suddenly a light from heaven flashed around him; and he fell to the ground, and heard a voice saying to him, "Saul, Saul, why are you persecuting Me?" (*Acts 9:1-4*)

Date

Awe is a way of being in rapport with the mystery of all reality. The awe that we sense or ought to sense when standing in the presence of a human being is a moment of intuition for the likeness of God which is concealed in its essence. Not only man; even inanimate things stand in relation to the Creator. The secret of every being is the divine care and concern that are invested in it. Something is at stake in every event.

Awe is an intuition for the creaturely dignity of all things and their preciousness to God; a realization that things not only are what they are but also stand, however remotely, for something absolute. Awe is a sense for the transcendence, for the reference everywhere to Him who is beyond all things.

Abraham Heschel

God in Search of Man: A Philosophy of Judaism

REFLECTING ON YOUR LIFE

Reading the Moment

Reflecting on the Moment

Is there any passage of Scripture that comes to mind that sheds light on this moment?

Responding to the Moment

Reaching up prayerfully

Reaching out personally

Praise the Lord!
For it is good to sing praises to our God;
For it is pleasant and praise is becoming.
The Lord builds up Jerusalem;
He gathered the outcasts of Israel.
He heals the brokenhearted,
And binds up their wounds.
He counts the number of the stars;
He gives names to all of them.
Great is our Lord, and abundant in strength;
His understanding is infinite.
The Lord supports the afflicted;
He brings down the wicked to the ground.
Sing to the Lord with thanksgiving;
Sing praises to our God on the lyre.

(Psalm 147:1-7)

Date

Forfeit your sense of awe, let your conceit diminish your ability to revere, and the universe becomes a market place for you.

Abraham Heschel
God in Search of Man: A Philosophy of Judaism

REFLECTING ON YOUR LIFE

Reading the Moment

Reflecting on the Moment

Is there any passage of Scripture that comes to mind that sheds light on this moment?

Responding to the Moment

Reaching up prayerfully

Reaching out personally

Now the man had relations with his wife Eve, and she conceived and gave birth to Cain, and she said, "I have gotten a manchild with the help of the Lord." And again, she gave birth to his brother Abel. And Abel was a keeper of the flocks, but Cain was a tiller of the ground.

So it came about in the course of time that Cain brought an offering to the Lord of the fruit of the ground. And Abel, on his part also brought of the firstlings of his flock and of their fat portions. And the Lord had regard for Abel and for his offering; but for Cain and for his offering He had no regard. So Cain became very angry and his countenance fell.

Then the Lord said to Cain, "Why are you angry? And why has your countenance fallen? If you do well, will not your countenance be lifted up? And if you do not do well, sin is crouching at the door; and its desire is for you, but you must master it."

And Cain told Abel his brother. And it came about that they were in the field, that Cain rose up against Abel his brother and killed him. *(Genesis 4:1-8)*

Date

"This is the place of my song-dream, the place the music played to me," whispered the Rat, as if in a trance. "Here, in this holy place, here if anywhere, surely we shall find Him!"

Then suddenly the Mole felt a great Awe fall upon him, an awe that turned his muscles to water, bowed his head, and rooted his feet to the ground. It was no panic terror—indeed he felt wonderfully at peace and happy—but it was an awe that smote and held him and, without seeing, he knew it could only mean that some august Presence was very, very near.

Kenneth Grahame

The Wind in the Willows

REFLECTING ON YOUR LIFE

Reading the Moment

Reflecting on the Moment

Is there any passage of Scripture that comes to mind that sheds light on this moment?

Responding to the Moment

Reaching up prayerfully

Reaching out personally

Then Jacob departed from Beersheba and went toward Haran. And he came to a certain place and spent the night there, because the sun had set; and he took one of the stones of the place and put it under his head, and lay down in that place. And he had a dream, and behold, a ladder was set on the earth with its top reaching to heaven; and behold, the angels of God were ascending and descending on it. . . . Then Jacob awoke from his sleep and said, "Surely the Lord is in this place, and I did not know it." *(Genesis 28:10-12, 16)*

Date

I was suspended in quiet contemplation, like a light uniting all things, when I saw a flash of wonderful splendour. In the centre of the radiance was a rainbow of lucent reflections and colours, and over it another of equal grandeur. Above the upper arch stood the Cross, touched with purple and stained with blood, the nailholes visible. Within the arches shone the human form of my Lord, Christ Jesus, sending out rays of glory. He generously gave me strength to look upon His beauty, for this time I saw Him face to face!

Saint Rose of Lima, Peru (1586-1617)

quoted in *The Soul Afire*

REFLECTING ON YOUR LIFE

Reading the Moment

Reflecting on the Moment

Is there any passage of Scripture that comes to mind that sheds light on this moment?

Responding to the Moment

Reaching up prayerfully

Reaching out personally

I, John . . . was in the Spirit on the Lord's day, and I heard behind me a loud voice. . . . And I turned to see the voice that was speaking to me. . . . And when I saw Him, I fell at His feet as a dead man. And He laid His right hand upon me, saying, "Do not be afraid; I am the first and the last, and the living One; and I was dead, and behold, I am alive forevermore." *(Revelation 1:9, 10, 12, 17-18)*

MOMENTS IN CHURCH

One of the places we go to hear God's voice is church. Sometimes what we hear there comes through a Bible reading or a prayer, a sermon or a song. Paul tells us we are to come to church bringing something to share—a psalm, a teaching, a hymn (1 Corinthians 14:26; Ephesians 5:19).

And so the early church, when it came together, was something like a potluck meal. In today's church the dining is a little more formal. But whether it's casual or coat-and-tie, it's still the "food" we come for.

Most of that "food" today is prepared by professionals who meticulously plan the menu and precisely measure the servings, so most of the luck is taken out of the pot, which sometimes is for the better. Though not always.

But whether your church is a five-star restaurant or more of a soup kitchen, it's not the ambiance of the location that counts, it's the nutrition of the food that's served there. And sometimes the simpler the fare, the better it is for the soul.

We come to church, or *should* come, not just to be fed but to feed, to give as well as receive, to speak as well as to listen. What we speak and what we give and what we feed others with is something that God has first spoken to us, first given to us, first fed to us.

These moments when we feed others, or when by others we are fed, are sometimes moments of transcendence. Moments when we are lifted above the care-worn shoulders of our own world and given a look through the transom into the world of another person, and every once in a while even given a glimpse into the world beyond.

Somebody's haltingly told story, for example, punctuated by tears.

A person kneeling in prayer.

A baby asleep in its mother's arms.

Communion.

These are the moments that make a difference not only in the service but in our lives. This week, when you're in church, see if there's not such a moment for you to receive . . . or maybe such a moment for you in some way to give.

Date *A Sunday, 1988*

If we stay at home by ourselves and read the Bible, we are going to miss a lot, for our reading will be unconsciously conditioned by our culture, limited by our ignorance, distorted by unnoticed prejudices. In worship we are part of "the large congregation" where all the writers of Scripture address us, where hymn writers use music to express truths which touch us not only in our heads but in our hearts, where the preacher who has just lived through six days of doubt, hurt, faith and blessing with the worshipers, speaks the truth of Scripture in a language of the congregation's present experience. We want to hear what God says and what he says to us: worship is the place where our attention is centered on these personal and decisive words of God.

Eugene Peterson
A Long Obedience in the Same Direction

REFLECTING ON YOUR LIFE

Reading the Moment

Judy and I went to a different church today, to visit. It was different in every way from the church we were attending. It had folding chairs instead of padded pews. Drums and guitars instead of a bell choir. Casual dress instead of coat-and-tie. It was something of a culture shock for us. The people sitting near us looked as if they had been pulled off the street by the scruff of their neck and plopped into the service. They had tattoos, body parts that were pierced, hair that was dyed. And they were there praising God with all their hearts. Tears streamed from some of their faces. Some knelt. Some went forward after the service for prayer. The message was spoken not preached. It was honest and heartfelt, not manipulative. The entire focus of the service was on worshiping Jesus and helping the wounded.

Reflecting on the Moment

That evening in the church service was really a montage of moments shuffled together over a period of about an hour and a half. There were things that happened during that time that we didn't understand, and some things that we didn't agree with. But we agreed with this. The heart of the church was in the right place. And the heart was focused on loving God with all its strength and its neighbor as itself. That was clear. I came away with a conviction that night that this must have been something of what the early church was like. People from all socio-economic groups huddled together around the cross of Christ, clinging to his feet with tears streaming down their faces, helping each other the best they could to love Him and to serve Him.

Is there any passage of Scripture that comes to mind that sheds light on this moment?

For consider your calling, brethren, that there were not many wise according to the flesh, not many mighty, not many noble; but God has chosen the foolish things of the world to shame the wise. (1 Cor. 1:26-27)

Responding to the Moment

Reaching up prayerfully

Dear God, I confess how critical I am sometimes, even in worldly worship, that sacred time when my eyes should be on you & not like the Pharisee who looked to those around him, comparing himself to others and boasting of his superiority. Keep me from doing that, Lord, either morally or theologically. For I am no different from the biker with the leather jacket and tattoos. We are all of us only sinners in need of your mercy.

Reaching out personally

I resolve not to let anything distract me from worshiping Christ. Not the choir or the lack of one. Not the organ, however off-key, or the drums, however loud. Not the mannerisms of the pastor or the shortcomings of his sermon. Not the person sitting next to me or the stiffness of the chair I'm seated on. Not the liturgy in the service or the looseness of the service.

Let us consider how to stimulate one another to love and good deeds, not forsaking our own assembling together, as is the habit of some, but encouraging one another; and all the more, as you see the day drawing near. (*Hebrews 10:24-25*)

Date

[Christ] works on us in all sorts of ways. . . . He works through Nature, through our own bodies, through books, sometimes through experiences which seem (at least at the time) *anti*-Christian. . . . But above all, He works on us through each other.

C.S. Lewis
Mere Christianity

REFLECTING ON YOUR LIFE

Reading the Moment

Reflecting on the Moment

Is there any passage of Scripture that comes to mind that sheds light on this moment?

Responding to the Moment

Reaching up prayerfully

Reaching out personally

Be devoted to one another. (*Romans 12:10*)

Love one another. (*Romans 13:8*)

Accept one another. (*Romans 15:7*)

Admonish one another. (*Romans 15:14*)

Care for one another. (*1 Corinthians 12:25*)

Be kind to one another. (*Ephesians 4:32*)

Comfort one another. (*1 Thessalonians 4:18*)

Encourage one another. (*1 Thessalonians 5:11*)

Date

In a true dialogue the preacher cannot stay on the outside. He cannot remain untouchable and invulnerable. . . .

When this dialogue takes place, those who listen will come to the recognition of who they really are since the words of the preacher will find a sounding board in their own hearts and find anchor places in their personal life-experiences. And when they allow his words to come so close as to become their flesh and blood, they can say: "What you say loudly, I whispered in the dark; what you pronounce so clearly, I had some suspicion about; what you put in the foreground, I felt in the back of my mind; what you hold so firmly in your hand always slipped away through my fingers. Yes, I find myself in your words because your words come from the depths of human experiences and, therefore, are not just yours but also mine, and your insights do not just belong to you, but are mine as well."

When a man who listens to a preacher can say this, there is a real dialogue. And if he were a little more spontaneous than most of us, he would say, "Yes, brother, you said it. Yes, Amen Alleluia." Only then is man able to recognize real dialogue and affirm his real self and come to the confession not only of his deficiencies and mistakes but also of himself as a man in desperate need for the Word of God which has the power to make him free.

Henri Nouwen
Creative Ministry

REFLECTING ON YOUR LIFE

Reading the Moment

Reflecting on the Moment

Is there any passage of Scripture that comes to mind that sheds light on this moment?

Responding to the Moment

Reaching up prayerfully

Reaching out personally

Paul had decided to sail past Ephesus in order that he might not have to spend time in Asia; for he was hurrying to be in Jerusalem, if possible, on the day of Pentecost. And from Miletus he sent to Ephesus and called to him the elders of the church. And when they had come to him, he said to them, "You yourselves know, from the first day that I set foot in Asia, how I was with you the whole time, serving the Lord with humility and with tears and with trials which came upon me through the plots of the Jews; how I did not shrink from declaring to you anything that was profitable, and teaching you publicly from house to house. . . .

And when he had said these things, he knelt down and prayed with them all. And they began to weep aloud and embraced Paul, and repeatedly kissed him, grieving especially over the word which he had spoken that they should see his face no more. And they were accompanying him to the ship. (*Acts 20:16-20, 36-38*)

Date

Little is gained without the spirit, and the spirit cannot be maintained by separated individuals. Therefore the Church or something like it must be cherished, criticized, nourished, and reformed. The Church of Jesus Christ, with all its blemishes, its divisions, and its failures, remains our best hope of spiritual vitality. However poor it is, life without it is worse.

Elton Trueblood
The Company of the Committed

REFLECTING ON YOUR LIFE

Reading the Moment

Reflecting on the Moment

Is there any passage of Scripture that comes to mind that sheds light on this moment?

Responding to the Moment

Reaching up prayerfully

Reaching out personally

For even as the body is one and yet has many members, and all the members of the body, though they are many, are one body, so also is Christ. For by one Spirit we were all baptized into one body, whether Jews or Greeks, whether slaves or free, and we were all made to drink of one Spirit. For the body is not one member, but many. If the foot should say, "Because I am not a hand, I am not a part of the body," it is not for this reason any the less a part of the body. And if the ear should say, "Because I am not an eye, I am not a part of the body," it is not for this reason any the less a part of the body. If the whole body were an eye, where would the hearing be? If the whole were hearing, where would the sense of smell be? But now God has placed the members, each one of them, in the body, just as He desired. And if they were all one member, where would the body be? But now there are many members, but one body. And the eye cannot say to the hand, "I have no need of you"; or again the head to the feet, "I have no need of you." On the contrary, it is much truer that the members of the body which seem to be weaker are necessary; and those members of the body, which we deem less honorable, on these we bestow more abundant honor, and our unseemly members come to have more abundant seemliness, whereas our seemly members have no need of it. But God has so composed the body, giving more abundant honor to that member which lacked, that there should be no division in the body, but that the members should have the same care for one another.
(1 Corinthians 12:12-25)

Date

Why do Christians sing when they are together? The reason is, quite simply, because in singing together it is possible for them to speak and pray the same Word at the same time; in other words, because here they can unite in the Word. All devotion, all attention should be concentrated upon the Word in the hymn. The fact that our spoken words are inadequate to express what we want to say, that the burden of our song goes far beyond all human words. Yet we do not hum a melody; we sing words of praise to God, words of thanksgiving, confession, and prayer. Thus the music is completely the servant of the Word. It elucidates the Word in its mystery.

Dietrich Bonhoeffer
Life Together

REFLECTING ON YOUR LIFE

Reading the Moment

Reflecting on the Moment

Is there any passage of Scripture that comes to mind that sheds light on this moment?

Responding to the Moment

Reaching up prayerfully

Reaching out personally

Let the word of Christ richly dwell within you, with all wisdom teaching and admonishing one another with psalms and hymns and spiritual songs, singing with thankfulness in your hearts to God. *(Colossians 3:16)*

Date

In Saskatoon, as God moved and expressed His will to church members, I guided them to share with the other members of the body. We could not adjust our lives to God if we did not know what He was saying. When the Head spoke to any member, all of us had to listen and hear what He said to our church. All were given an opportunity and encouraged to share. Each was encouraged to respond as God guided him or her. This happened not only in worship (usually at the close of the service), but also in prayer meetings, committee meetings, business meetings, Sunday School classes, home Bible studies, and personal conversations. Many called the church office and shared what God was saying to them in their quiet times. Still others shared what they experienced at work or at school. The entire church became experientially and practically aware of Christ's presence in our midst.

Henry T. Blackaby and Claude V. King
Experiencing God

REFLECTING ON YOUR LIFE

Reading the Moment

Reflecting on the Moment

Is there any passage of Scripture that comes to mind that sheds light on this moment?

Responding to the Moment

Reaching up prayerfully

Reaching out personally

Speaking the truth in love, we are to grow up in all aspects into Him, who is the head, even Christ, from whom the whole body, being fitted and held together by that which every joint supplies, according to the proper working of each individual part, causes the growth of the body for the building up of itself in love. *(Ephesians 4:15-16)*

MOMENTS WITH THE ARTS

In some circles of the church today and in some centuries of church history, the arts have been looked at suspiciously if not scornfully. But like the tarnished image of God in every human being, the tarnish is not all there is to our humanness. Underneath our fallenness is the gloriousness from which we have fallen. And if only we have the eyes to see, something of that gloriousness glints through the verdegris that covers us all.

To be sure, the arts have given us plenty of reasons to be skeptical of them, even critical of them. But they have given us something else.

They have given us moments.

Acclaimed screenwriter Robert Towne once said, "A movie, I think, is really only four or five moments between two people; the rest of it exists to give those moments their impact and resonance."

There are moments within us so joyful that dancing comes closer to capturing the feeling than anything else. There are moments so tragic that nothing but drama could begin to describe the ache. There are moments so peaceful only the rhythms of a gentle musical score could convey the feeling. There are moments so lovely only the delicate hands of a sonnet could hold its loveliness without crushing it. There are moments so fleeting only a painting could still it long enough to be touched.

Through dance, through drama, through music, through poetry, through art, the soul expresses itself. With a passionate but sometimes unsteady hand, the arts trace the distant shores of the soul, mapping its uncharted reaches, with all its promises of gold and its warnings of dragons.

The map may be marked with sightings of mermaids, which in reality were only seals basking on the rocks, seen through the eyes of delirious and sun-struck sailors. The map may be noted with superstitious symbols at its edges to steer ships away from falling off the flat surface of the earth. The map is not infallible. But it does offer direction. And it can help in our search for God and for each other and for ourselves, which is sometimes the most scary and uncertain search.

Like all searches, now and then it comes up empty-handed or with hands filled with less than we expected, but often the North on the map turns out to be true North or very close to it. And though the map may not lead us home, it may help us get our bearings.

What keeps us coming back to the arts, in spite of the disappointments, is hope. Not only the hope of touching something just out of our reach, but the hope of being touched in return. Not only the hoping of finding something, but the hope of being found. Not only the hope of loving, but the hope of being loved.

Sometimes it is the love of God that finds us there, touches us there. Through the play *Les Misérables*, maybe. Or maybe through a poignant phrase of a Simon and Garfunkel song. Or a crayoned picture taped to the refrigerator door.

Take some time this week to treat yourself to a few moments in the arts. That might be a walk through the landscape art of a botanical garden or a visit to a music store to listen to a new CD on headphones. Wherever it is you go, see if there isn't some moment there that moves you. Note where it moves you. And why.

Date Jan. 10, 1998

[Drama] gives the essence of life, and in three hours it speaks volumes. It warns and counsels, teaches justice and keeps alive pity. It celebrates man's liberty and his struggles, and all that is noble wanders into it. It enlists the sympathies to such an extent that the listener is his own poet. It analyzes all motives, withholding nothing, lays bare everything. It is in fact the plainest, most direct of all forms of teaching. It does not formulate morals in words, but in deeds; and if life, which is the drama, is not a constant mentor, unheeded also in its teachings, what is it?

W.T. Price

The Technique of Drama

REFLECTING ON YOUR LIFE

Reading the Moment

Saw the movie, <u>Titanic</u>, which prompted me to rent the video, <u>A Night to Remember</u>, an earlier version of the 1912 disaster. Several scenes leapt out at me, all involving the <u>California</u>, a ship that was only an hour away. It was close enough to come to Titanic's aid and rescue all on board if it had responded to the distress signals that were sent both by sky rockets and by wireless. Tragically, the people on board failed to see or hear the distress signals, resulting in the loss over 2/3 of the Titanic's passengers and crew.

Reflecting on the Moment

The tragedy of the Titanic is so epic it seems a parable of sorts for all of us who live in an era of technological marvels. The main lesson of the parable seems clear enough — how pride comes before the fall, or, in this case, before the sinking. The pride of man's mastery over his environment, causing him to go "full steam ahead" in spite of the warnings of icebergs, is what led to the collision. The pride of thinking the ship was "unsinkable" is what led to the decision not to put enough lifeboats on board. But the scenes involving the California teach another lesson. The men on board had seen the sky rockets in the distance, but they took them for the fireworks of a celebration, not a distress signal. The radio operator had taken off his headphones and gone to sleep, missing the Titanic's SOS. All this underscores to me the importance of being attentive & responsive to the distress signals around me.

Is there any passage of Scripture that comes to mind that sheds light on this moment?

Pride goes before the fall. (Prov.)
You have ears but do not hear, and eyes but do not see (somewhere in O.T.)
"Lord, when did we see you hungry or thirsty or in prison?" (Matt. 25)

Responding to the Moment

Reaching up prayerfully

Please, God, help me to be awake and alert at my post as a husband, as a father, and as a friend. Help me to be able to recognize the distress signals that are going out all around me. Help me be quick to hear, diligent to see, and swift to respond.

Reaching out personally

Who are some of the people around me that are sending out distress signals for help?

① A letter came from someone who is struggling with the moral equivalent of a brush with an iceberg. I should call, not ~~write~~ write. And soon. Try to help the best I can.

② Question — Is my body sending out distress signals that I've been missing? Some trouble sleeping.

③ A boy who's a friend of our kids has a mother dying of cancer. He's very quiet so I need to be especially alert for distress signals. Keep him in my prayers. Think of ways to help him and his dad. Include him with some family things, invite him over, etc.

To you, O men, I call,
And my voice is to the sons of men.
O naive ones, discern prudence;
And, O fools, discern wisdom.

(Proverbs 8:4-5)

Date

One artist imagines himself the creator of an autonomous spiritual world; he hoists upon his shoulders the act of creating this world and of populating it, together with the total responsibility for it. . . .

Another artist recognizes above himself a higher power and joyfully works as a humble apprentice under God's heaven, though graver and more demanding still is his responsibility for all he writes or paints—and for the souls which apprehend it. However, it was not he who created this world, nor does he control it; there can be no doubts about its foundations. It is merely given to the artist to sense more keenly than others the harmony of the world, the beauty and ugliness of man's role in it—and to vividly communicate this to mankind. . . .

Archaeologists have yet to discover an earthly stage of human existence when we possessed no art. In the twilight preceding the dawn of mankind we received it from Hands which we did not have a chance to see clearly. *Why* this gift for us? How should we treat it? . . . .

Not everything can be named. Some things draw us beyond words. Art can warm even a chilled and sunless soul to an exalted spiritual experience. Through art we occasionally receive—indistinctly, briefly—revelations the likes of which cannot be achieved by rational thought.

It is like that small mirror of legend: you look into it but instead of yourself you glimpse for a moment the Inaccessible, a realm forever beyond reach. And your soul begins to ache.

Aleksandr I. Solzhenitsyn
"The Nobel Lecture on Literature"
East and West

REFLECTING ON YOUR LIFE

Reading the Moment

Reflecting on the Moment

Is there any passage of Scripture that comes to mind that sheds light on this moment?

Responding to the Moment

Reaching up prayerfully

Reaching out personally

Now the Lord spoke to Moses, saying, "See, I have called by name Bezalel, the son of Uri, the son of Hur, of the tribe of Judah. And I have filled him with the Spirit of God in wisdom, in understanding, in knowledge, and in all kinds of craftsmanship, to make artistic designs for work in gold, in silver, and in bronze, and in the cutting of stones for settings, and in the carving of wood, that he make work in all kinds of craftsmanship. And behold, I Myself have appointed with him Oholiab, the son of Ahisamach, of the tribe of Dan; and in the hearts of all who are skillful I have put skill, that they may make all that I have commanded you: the tent of meeting, and the ark of testimony, and the mercy seat upon it, and all the furniture of the tent, the table also and its utensils, and the pure gold lampstand with all its utensils, and the altar of incense, the altar of burnt offering also with all its utensils, and the laver and its stand, the woven garments as well, and the holy garments for Aaron the priest, and the garments of his sons, with which to carry on their priesthood; the anointing oil also, and the fragrant incense for the holy place, they are to make them according to all that I have commanded you." (*Exodus 31:1-11*)

Date

Music is, in the first place, the voice of God to the soul. There are other ways, my friends, of preaching the Gospel than by speaking from a pulpit. . . .

   And music is, in the second place, the voice of the heart's aspirations towards God. It is the speech of the spirit, the language of the soul. What we cannot utter, but only dimly feel, that music seems to say for us. It is the voice of our unshaped and unspoken prayers.

Reverend Canon Shuttleworth
quoted in *Self Culture for Young People*, edited by Andrew Sloan Draper

REFLECTING ON YOUR LIFE

Reading the Moment

Reflecting on the Moment

Is there any passage of Scripture that comes to mind that sheds light on this moment?

Responding to the Moment

Reaching up prayerfully

Reaching out personally

Praise the Lord!
Praise God in His sanctuary;
Praise Him in His mighty expanse.
Praise Him for His mighty deeds;
Praise Him according to His excellent greatness.

Praise Him with trumpet sound;
Praise Him with harp and lyre.
Praise Him with timbrel and dancing;
Praise Him with stringed instruments and pipe.
Praise Him with loud cymbals;
Praise Him with resounding cymbals.
Let everything that has breath praise the Lord.
Praise the Lord!
(*Psalm 150*)

After these things I looked, and behold, a door standing open in heaven, and the first voice which I heard, like the sound of a trumpet speaking with me, said, "Come up here, and I will show you what must take place after these things." (*Revelation 4:1*)

Date

Stories enlarge us, help resolve fears, restore us as particular, distinctive individuals with as yet unrealized dreams. Stories can activate our inner power to choose goodness, vitality, and love. Saint Paul described these higher experiential realms. He prayed (and I paraphrase here) that the eyes of our heart might become enlightened that we might know what is the hope of God's calling for us.

Most people, however, seem to prefer safety. They shun the exhilarating heights of their own advanced awareness. Watching films alertly gives us a way to inch toward the truth.

Marsha Sinetar
Reel Power: Spiritual Growth Through Film

REFLECTING ON YOUR LIFE

Reading the Moment

Reflecting on the Moment

Is there any passage of Scripture that comes to mind that sheds light on this moment?

Responding to the Moment

Reaching up prayerfully

Reaching out personally

And behold, a certain lawyer stood up and put Him to the test, saying, "Teacher, what shall I do to inherit eternal life?"

And He said to him, "What is written in the Law? How does it read to you?"

And he answered and said, "You shall love the Lord your God with all your heart, and with all your soul, and with all your strength, and with all your mind; and your neighbor as yourself."

And He said to him, "You have answered correctly; do this, and you will live."

But wishing to justify himself, he said to Jesus, "And who is my neighbor?"

Jesus replied and said, "A certain man was going down from Jerusalem to Jericho; and he fell among robbers, and they stripped him and beat him, and went off leaving him half dead. And by chance a certain priest was going down on that road, and when he saw him, he passed by on the other side. And likewise a Levite also, when he came to the place and saw him, passed by on the other side. But a certain Samaritan, who was on a journey, came upon him; and when he saw him, he felt compassion, and came to him, and bandaged up his wounds, pouring oil and wine on them; and he put him on his own beast, and brought him to an inn, and took care of him. And on the next day he took out two denarii and gave them to the innkeeper and said, 'Take care of him; and whatever more you spend, when I return, I will repay you.' Which of these three do you think proved to be a neighbor to the man who fell into the robbers' hands?"

And he said, "The one who showed mercy toward him."

And Jesus said to him, "Go and do the same." (*Luke 10:25-37*)

Date

Our attraction to characters in stories is largely the same no matter what their source—literature, history, contemporary culture, family, or our own lives. In each case we are drawn to tales of fellow human beings facing choices that remind us of our own, or at the least prompt us to ask, "What would I do if . . . ?"

And in that question lies not only our humanity but also the potential for our own character to be formed by the characters in our stories. For while that question—"What should I do?"—hangs in the air, who we are is up for grabs. Answering the question does not simply entail discovering who we are but allows us in part to determine who we are. Every powerful character we encounter in story is a challenge to our own character, and holds the possibility of changing us.

Daniel Taylor
The Healing Power of Stories

REFLECTING ON YOUR LIFE

Reading the Moment

Reflecting on the Moment

Is there any passage of Scripture that comes to mind that sheds light on this moment?

Responding to the Moment

Reaching up prayerfully

Reaching out personally

Then the Lord sent Nathan to David. And he came to him, and said,
    "There were two men in one city, the one rich and the other poor.
    The rich man had a great many flocks and herds.
    But the poor man had nothing except one little ewe lamb
    Which he bought and nourished;
    And it grew up together with him and his children.
    It would eat of his bread and drink of his cup and lie in his bosom,
    And was like a daughter to him.
    Now a traveler came to the rich man,
    And he was unwilling to take from his own flock or his own herd,
    To prepare for the wayfarer who had come to him;
    Rather he took the poor man's ewe lamb and prepared it for the man
        who had come to him."
    Then David's anger burned greatly against the man and he said to Nathan, "As the Lord lives, surely the man who has done this deserves to die. And he must make restitution for the lamb fourfold, because he did this thing and had no compassion."
    Nathan then said to David, "You are the man!" *(2 Samuel 12:1-7)*

Date

Faces are not permanently beautiful to us, nor are landscapes. There seem to be moments of revelation, moments when we see in the transition of one part to another the unification of the whole. There is a sense of comprehension and of great happiness. We have entered into a great order and have been carried into greater knowledge by it. This sometimes in a passing face, a landscape, a growing thing. We may call it a passage into another dimension than our ordinary. If one could but record the vision of these moments by some sort of sign! It was in this hope that the arts were invented. Signposts on the way to what may be. Signposts toward greater knowledge.

Robert Henri
The Art Spirit

REFLECTING ON YOUR LIFE

Reading the Moment

Reflecting on the Moment

Is there any passage of Scripture that comes to mind that sheds light on this moment?

Responding to the Moment

Reaching up prayerfully

Reaching out personally

How beautiful you are, my darling,
How beautiful you are!
Your eyes are like doves behind your veil;
Your hair is like a flock of goats
That have descended from Mount Gilead.
Your teeth are like a flock of newly shorn ewes
Which have come up from their washing,
All of which bear twins,
And not one among them has lost her young.
Your lips are like a scarlet thread,
And your mouth is lovely.
Your temples are like a slice of a pomegranate
Behind your veil. . . .
You are altogether beautiful, my darling,
And there is no blemish in you. . . .
You have made my heart beat faster with a single
glance of your eyes.

(Song of Solomon 4:1-3, 7, 9)

MOMENTS OF JOY

My childhood images of heaven seem, now as I look back on them, like an underdeveloped photograph. A hazy place in the clouds with colors washed out by diffused light. People walking around in long white robes. Their faces, calm and sedate. Their conversations, serious and important. There was no running in heaven, at least none that I could imagine. Certainly no playing. I never imagined laughter there. Or excitement. Or anything really very good to eat.

And all that for all eternity!

Hardly the travel brochure that would excite anyone to want to visit there, let alone to move there.

Since none of us *has* gone there, we are left largely to our imaginations to visualize what heaven is like. And our imaginations have been influenced largely by our popular culture, from movies like *Ghost* to television shows like "Touched by an Angel" to figurines like Precious Moments.

We have been left with more than our imaginations, though. We have been left with the revelations of a few people who have actually seen heaven and lived to tell about it. Isaiah was one of them (Isaiah 6). The Apostle Paul was another (2 Corinthians 12:1-7). The disciple John was still another (Revelation 19–22). The revelations were so dazzling, they overwhelmed each one of them.

If that is true and if it is also true that "eye has not seen and ear has not heard . . . all that God has prepared for those who love Him" (1 Corinthians 2:9), then whatever else heaven is, it is more than our experience of life here on earth, not less. It is the fullness of life, not its reduction. It is the waking, as C.S. Lewis put it, not the dream.

From the glimpses of heaven given us by Jesus, we know that whatever else heaven is, it is full of joy. "Joy" is the term He used to describe the atmosphere there when just one sinner repents (Luke 15:7, 10), and the picture He left us with is one of merriment, of music, dancing, and feasting (vv. 22-25). "Enter into the joy of your master," are the words He used in a parable to describe the rewards of heaven (Matthew 25:21, 23).

Now and then we get firefly glimpses of that joy, a phosphorescent blip of something that draws us to faraway fields. Fleeting moments that pass all understanding. Here one second, someplace else the next. With childlike excitement we follow them, hoping to catch one of them long enough to take in the wonder of it all.

C.S. Lewis describes the feeling as an "inconsolable longing." In those moments of longing our joy speaks to us. It speaks to us the way the lick of the spoon speaks of birthday cake, the way the smell of roasting turkey speaks of the Thanksgiving meal, the way the scent of pine speaks of Christmas.

And what it speaks of, is heaven.

Date **August 17, 1988**

I do not think that the life of Heaven bears any analogy to play or dance in respect of frivolity. I do think that while we are in this "valley of tears," cursed with labour, hemmed round with necessities, tripped up with frustrations, doomed to perpetual plannings, puzzlings and anxieties, certain qualities that must belong to the celestial condition have no chance to get through, can project no image of themselves, except in activities which, for us here and now, are frivolous. . . . Dance and game are frivolous, unimportant down here; for "down here" is not their natural place. Here, they are a moment's rest from the life we were placed here to live. But in this world everything is upside down. That which, if it could be prolonged here, would be a truancy, is likest that which in a better country is the End of ends. Joy is the serious business of Heaven.

C.S. Lewis
Letters to Malcolm

REFLECTING ON YOUR LIFE

Reading the Moment

Shubert Theatre. Los Angeles. Went to see the stage play, Les Misérables, with some friends. It was a deeply religious story at its core, a story contrasting Law and Grace. Several songs brought tears as well as applause. At the end of the story everyone was on their feet, clapping hard, tears streaming down the faces of many, including mine. Why? It was the end of the life of the main character, Jean Valjean, who passes through the veil that separates this life from the next. The cast comes on stage and sings in a crescendo of emotion about living in freedom in the garden of the Lord: "Will you join in our crusade? Who will be strong and stand with me? Somewhere beyond the barricade, is there a world you long to see?"

Reflecting on the Moment

There in that theater were people of all ages, all kinds of backgrounds, and in all stages of belief and disbelief. And there they were standing, applauding, weeping. The moment seemed a collective prayer of some kind. "Please, God, if there is a world beyond the barricade of this one, please show us a glimpse of it, take our hand and lead us there. Please."

That night at the theater I was moved many times, to tears sometimes, to my feet other times. That night at the end of the play I was given a glimpse of that world beyond the barricade. And Heaven seemed somehow not only more real... but more wonderful.

Is there any passage of Scripture that comes to mind that sheds light on this moment?

For our citizenship is in heaven, from which also we eagerly wait for a savior, the Lord Jesus Christ. (Phil. 3:20)

Responding to the Moment

Reaching up prayerfully

Thank you, God, for the hope of Heaven. Thank you that there a place has been prepared for me there. Thank you that the place is real and that the hope is true. Thank you, too, for that moment at the end of Les Miserables, where that my heart was stirred by the fleeting glimpse I saw of life behind the veil.

Reaching out personally

Jean Valjean's life was a life of kindness. That's why the scene of him dying at the end of the play was so powerful. He was missed because he was loved. And he was loved because he touched so many people while he was on earth. I want that kind of life. Not fame, Not some kind of literary immortality. But a life of kindness. Lived a day at a time, a moment at a time.

Let Israel be glad in his Maker;
Let the sons of Zion rejoice in their King.
Let them praise His name with dancing;
Let them sing praises to Him with timbrel and lyre.
For the Lord takes pleasure in His people.

(Psalm 149:2-4a)

Date

God whispers to us in our pleasures. . . .

C.S. Lewis
The Problem of Pain

At the end of the service, Jennie told him, "Your mind's not with us any more, Eric. It's full of running and starting and medals and pace. Your head's so full of running you've no room for standing still."

"Jennie, Jennie, don't fret yourself," Eric said gently.

"I do fret myself. I'm frightened for you. I'm frightened for what it all might do to you."

A young schoolgirl approached Eric to ask for his autograph.

"Do you want to pick yourself a pen?" Eric asked humorously, crouching over so the schoolgirl could select a pen from his jacket pocket. He quickly signed his name in the girl's autograph book. "There you are."

The girl gave him a look of open hero-worship. "Thanks, Mr. Liddell."

Eric went back to Jennie. "Come on, let's go for a walk. I've got something to say."

They walked out of Edinburgh far enough up a hillside to overlook the ancient city. The grey rooftops appeared like stepping stones leading to the great castle jutting out against the skyline.

"It's a sight and a half, isn't it, Jennie?" said Eric, staring back. "I'll be sad to leave it." He moved closer to her. "I've decided. I'm going back to China. The missionary service has accepted me."

Jennie hugged him. "Oh, Eric, I'm so pleased."

Eric said quietly. "But I've got a lot of running to do first." Her look of happiness vanished. "Jennie, Jennie, you've got to understand. I believe that God made me for a purpose. For China. But He also made me fast, and when I run I feel His pleasure."

Chariots of Fire
W.J. Weatherby, based on a
screenplay by Colin Welland

REFLECTING ON YOUR LIFE

Reading the Moment

Reflecting on the Moment

Is there any passage of Scripture that comes to mind that sheds light on this moment?

Responding to the Moment

Reaching up prayerfully

Reaching out personally

His delight is not in the strength of the horse,
nor His pleasure in the legs of a man;
But the Lord takes pleasure in those who fear Him,
in those who hope in His steadfast love.

(Psalm 147:10-11, my paraphrase)

Date

Joy is essential to the spiritual life. Whatever we may think or say about God, when we are not joyful, our thoughts and words cannot bear fruit. Jesus reveals to us God's love so that his joy may become ours and that our joy may become complete. Joy is the experience of knowing that you are unconditionally loved and that nothing—sickness, failure, emotional distress, oppression, war, or even death—can take that love away. . . .

Still, nothing happens automatically in the spiritual life. Joy does not simply happen to us. We have to choose joy and keep choosing it every day. It is a choice based on the knowledge that we belong to God and have found in God our refuge and our safety and that nothing, not even death, can take God away from us. . . .

It is important to become aware that at every moment of our life we have an opportunity to choose joy. Life has many sides to it. There are always sorrowful and joyful sides to the reality we live. And so we always have a choice to live in the moment as a cause for resentment or as a cause for joy. It is in the choice that our true freedom lies, and that freedom is, in the final analysis, the freedom to love.

It might be a good idea to ask ourselves how we develop our capacity to choose joy. Maybe we could spend a moment at the end of each day and decide to remember that day—whatever may have happened—as a day to be grateful for. In so doing we increase our heart's capacity to choose for joy. And as our hearts become more joyful, we will become, without any special effort, a source of joy for others. Just as sadness begets sadness, so joy begets joy.

Henri Nouwen
Here and Now

REFLECTING ON YOUR LIFE

Reading the Moment

Reflecting on the Moment

Is there any passage of Scripture that comes to mind that sheds light on this moment?

Responding to the Moment

Reaching up prayerfully

Reaching out personally

Rejoice in the Lord always; again I will say, rejoice! (*Philippians 4:4*)

Date

The voice we should listen to most as we choose a vocation is the voice that we might think we should listen to least, and that is the voice of our gladness. What can we do that makes us the gladdest, what can we do that leaves us with the strongest sense of sailing true north and of peace, which is much of what gladness is? Is it making things with our hands out of wood or stone or paint on canvas? Or is it making something we hope like truth out of words? Or is it making people laugh or weep in a way that cleanses their spirit? I believe that if it is a thing that makes us truly glad, then it is a good thing and it is our thing and it is the calling voice that we were made to answer with our lives.

And also, where we are most needed. In a world where there is so much drudgery, so much grief, so much emptiness and fear and pain, our gladness in our work is as much needed as we ourselves need to be glad. If we keep our eyes and ears open, our hearts open, we will find the place surely.

Frederick Buechner
The Hungering Dark

REFLECTING ON YOUR LIFE

Reading the Moment

Reflecting on the Moment

Is there any passage of Scripture that comes to mind that sheds light on this moment?

Responding to the Moment

Reaching up prayerfully

Reaching out personally

I will bless the Lord who has counseled me;
Indeed, my mind instructs me in the night.
I have set the Lord continually before me;
Because He is at my right hand, I will not be shaken.
Therefore my heart is glad, and my glory rejoices;
My flesh also will dwell securely.
For Thou wilt not abandon my soul to Sheol;
Neither wilt Thou allow Thy Holy One to undergo decay.
Thou wilt make known to me the path of life;
In Thy presence is fulness of joy;
In Thy right hand there are pleasures forever.

(Psalm 16:7-11)

Date

I found out from working with the sisters that they are just who they appear to be. I have a lot of daily contact with them, doing the ordinary things we do, like working in the kitchen and scrubbing the floors, serving meals, driving to the supermarket and then taking people to the doctor or to a psychiatric unit in the hospital, and dealing sometimes with some very unpleasant people along the way. And they are always so cheerful. It's not the gritted-teeth cheerfulness, it's the real thing.

I'm convinced that the external cheerfulness is the manifestation of an inward joy that they feel. I know that anyone who works with them is aware of the time they spend in the chapel on their knees, and they are very happy because of it. Their happiest time is when they pray—they look forward to it, they are eager to pray and to refuel and they are equally eager to come out of that refueling and give away the energy that they receive. This is not a fanaticism, it is a genuine joyful desire to share what they have. Just as they don't keep any of the material things that they have: anything that's given to them, clothing or food or money or whatever it may be—paper bags, rubber bands, you name it— they give it away. Everything that comes in goes out.

A volunteer at a Missionary of Charity home in London
quoted in *A Simple Path* by Mother Teresa
compiled by Lucinda Vardey

REFLECTING ON YOUR LIFE

Reading the Moment

Reflecting on the Moment

Is there any passage of Scripture that comes to mind that sheds light on this moment?

Responding to the Moment

Reaching up prayerfully

Reaching out personally

Serve the Lord with gladness;
Come before Him with joyful singing.

(Psalm 100:2)

Date

The settled happiness and security which we all desire, God withholds from us by the very nature of the world: but joy, pleasure, merriment, He has scattered broadcast. We are never safe, but we have plenty of fun, and some ecstasy. It is not hard to see why. The security we crave would teach us to rest our hearts in this world and [pose] an obstacle to our return to God: a few moments of happy love, a landscape, a symphony, a merry meeting with our friends, a [swim] or a football match, have no such tendency. Our Father refreshes us on the journey with some pleasant inns, but will not encourage us to mistake them for home.

C.S. Lewis
The Problem of Pain

REFLECTING ON YOUR LIFE

Reading the Moment

Reflecting on the Moment

Is there any passage of Scripture that comes to mind that sheds light on this moment?

Responding to the Moment

Reaching up prayerfully

Reaching out personally

Here is what I have seen to be good and fitting: to eat, to drink and enjoy oneself in all one's labor in which he toils under the sun during the few years of his life which God has given him; for this is his reward.

Go then, eat your bread in happiness, and drink your wine with a cheerful heart; for God has already approved your works.

Enjoy life with the woman whom you love all the days of your fleeting life which He has given to you under the sun; for this is your reward in life.
(Ecclesiastes 5:18; 9:7, 9)

Moments of Tears

We cry for all sorts of reasons. When we're happy. When we're sad. When we're frustrated. When we're angry. When we're scared. When we're in pain. When we see someone else in pain.

Though the chemical composition of those tears is the same, their meaning is not.

Look up a word like *run* in the dictionary, for example, and you'll see that though the word is spelled the same in all its contexts, its meaning is different. A nose can run, and that is different from a run on a bank. And that is different from a run of salmon. And that is different from a home run. And that is different from something that is run-of-the-mill.

The tears that come to our eyes when we drop a can of beans on our foot are different from the tears that come to our eyes when we look at an old photograph and remember someone we love. And those tears are different from the ones that come to our eyes when we jump to our feet when the home team comes from behind to score the winning touchdown.

Tears are the language of the soul, and like any language, the meaning of its words are not determined by a dictionary definition but by the context in which the words are used. Sometimes the context of our tears or the tears of others lies deep within the memory of the soul. Tears have a way of taking us back in time to give attention to those memories, something in the past that needs healing, maybe, or forgiving, or understanding, or simply honoring by our grateful remembrance.

Though more difficult to define, tears are more expressive than words. They are also more difficult to hide behind than words, for what we weep over reveals who we are. Our tears pull back the curtain to reveal the identity of our true self, which is often kept from other people like a self-conscious secret.

154

Tears not only reveal our true self, they renew our soul, they restore us to one another, and sometimes in a watershed moment they even redirect the course of our life. Such is the power of tears.

And sometimes that power is harnessed by God as a moment of revelation.

About us.

About other people.

Even about God Himself.

Date *Spring, 1993*

You never know what may cause them. The sight of the Atlantic Ocean can do it, or a piece of music, or a face you've never seen before. A pair of somebody's old shoes can do it. Almost any movie made before the great sadness that came over the world after the Second World War, a horse cantering across a meadow, the high school basketball team running out onto the gym floor at the start of a game. You can never be sure. But of this you can be sure. Whenever you find tears in your eyes, especially unexpected tears, it is well to pay the closest attention.

They are not only telling you something about the secret of who you are, but more often than not God is speaking to you through them of the mystery of where you have come from and is summoning you to where, if your soul is to be saved, you should go next.

Frederick Buechner
Whistling in the Dark

REFLECTING ON YOUR LIFE

Reading the Moment

My daughter Kelly was graduating from middle school at a Christian school in southern California. I accompanied her to the banquet, honoring their passage into high school. It was a fairly formal affair with everyone dressed-up, taking pictures, things like that. When everyone was seated, one of the girls in the class walked to the microphone to say the blessing. She started a little shaky, her voice cracking, then pausing, and trying to start up again. It was an awkward moment, and my heart went out to her as I'm sure everyone else's did. "Please, God, help her get through this," I prayed. But she couldn't get through it. She was crying at the microphone until finally a school official came to her rescue and finished the prayer for her.

Reflecting on the Moment

It was at that moment that I knew how much the school had meant to that girl at the microphone — and to all the kids who went there, for when the prayer was finished others were wiping their eyes too. The tears of that girl that evening were more articulate and compelling than any promotional brochure I had read from the school. In those tears were distilled all the love, the friendships, the influence of the faculty, all the wonderful experiences that she was leaving behind. If I had ever ~~questioned~~ questioned whether this was a good place for my kids, I questioned no longer.

Is there any passage of Scripture that comes to mind that sheds light on this moment?

I can't think of any off hand.

Responding to the Moment

Reaching up prayerfully

Father, thank you for this school to which I have entrusted a portion of my children's lives. Thank you for the hard work and the ~~enthusiasm~~ dedication of all the teachers and the staff. Thank you for the friendships that are here and the experiences that they all have shared together, and that this is a place where the Lord Jesus is honored. Thank you for that.

Reaching out personally

Although my kids are at a different school in a different state, it is still a school where Christ is honored. I take that for granted. And I have been remiss in not expressing my appreciation. This week I will write the principal a note of appreciation, along with some notes for several of the teachers who have made a difference in my kids' lives.

Now one of the Pharisees was requesting Him to dine with him. And He entered the Pharisee's house, and reclined at the table. And behold, there was a woman in the city who was a sinner; and when she learned that He was reclining at the table in the Pharisee's house, she brought an alabaster vial of perfume, and standing behind Him at His feet, weeping, she began to wet His feet with her tears. (*Luke 7:36-38a*)

Date

The psalmists often wrote in tears, the prophets could hardly conceal their heavyheartedness, and the apostle Paul in his otherwise joyous epistle to the Philippians broke into tears when he thought of the many who were enemies of the cross of Christ and whose end was destruction. Those Christian leaders who shook the world were one and all men of sorrows whose witness to mankind welled out of heavy hearts: There is no power in tears per se, but tears and power ever lie close together in the Church of the First-born.

A.W. Tozer
God Tells the Man Who Cares

REFLECTING ON YOUR LIFE

Reading the Moment

Reflecting on the Moment

Is there any passage of Scripture that comes to mind that sheds light on this moment?

Responding to the Moment

Reaching up prayerfully

Reaching out personally

I am weary with my sighing;
Every night I make my bed swim,
I dissolve my couch with my tears.
My eye has wasted away with grief.

(Psalm 6:6-7a)

My eyes fail because of tears,
My spirit is greatly troubled;
My heart is poured out on the earth,
Because of the destruction of the daughter of my people,
When little ones and infants faint
In the streets of the city.

(Lamentations 2:11)

Brethren, join in following my example, and observe those who walk according to the pattern you have in us. For many walk, of whom I often told you, and now tell you even weeping, that they are enemies of the cross of Christ, whose end is destruction, whose god is their appetite, and whose glory is in their shame, who set their minds on earthly things.

(Philippians 3:17-19)

Date

There is no language more compelling and expressive than tears. Among all forms of communication, crying has the potential to express the greatest variety of messages with the most captivating effects.

Jeffrey A. Kottler
The Language of Tears

REFLECTING ON YOUR LIFE

Reading the Moment

Reflecting on the Moment

Is there any passage of Scripture that comes to mind that sheds light on this moment?

Responding to the Moment

Reaching up prayerfully

Reaching out personally

When Mary came where Jesus was, she saw Him, and fell at His feet, saying to Him, "Lord, if You had been here, my brother would not have died."

When Jesus therefore saw her weeping, and the Jews who came with her, also weeping, He was deeply moved in spirit, and was troubled, and said, "Where have you laid him?"

They said to Him, "Lord, come and see."

Jesus wept. And so the Jews were saying, "Behold how He loved him!"

(John 11:32-36)

Date

So much is distilled in our tears, not the least of which is wisdom in living life. From my own tears I have learned that if you follow your tears, you will find your heart. If you find your heart, you will find what is dear to God. And if you find what is dear to God, you will find the answer to how you should live your life.

Ken Gire
Windows of the Soul

REFLECTING ON YOUR LIFE

Reading the Moment

Reflecting on the Moment

Is there any passage of Scripture that comes to mind that sheds light on this moment?

Responding to the Moment

Reaching up prayerfully

Reaching out personally

Those who sow in tears shall reap with joyful shouting.
He who goes to and fro weeping, carrying his bag of seed,
Shall indeed come again with a shout of joy, bringing his sheaves with him.

(Psalm 126:5-6)

Date

In some ways, tearful experiences are magical. They represent those times when you are most moved, when you are most alive, in the sense that your head and your heart, your very spirit, are all synchronized in a single effort to communicate what is going on inside you.

Jeffrey A. Kottler
The Language of Tears

REFLECTING ON YOUR LIFE

Reading the Moment

Reflecting on the Moment

Is there any passage of Scripture that comes to mind that sheds light on this moment?

Responding to the Moment

Reaching up prayerfully

Reaching out personally

There is an appointed time for everything. And there is a time for every event under heaven—
A time to give birth, and a time to die;
A time to plant, and a time to uproot what is planted.
A time to kill, and a time to heal;
A time to tear down, and a time to build up.
A time to weep.
(Ecclesiastes 3:1-4a)

Date

Talk of tears, penitence, and confession is hard to take nowadays. Such things are considered by some to be both unfashionable and unhealthy. In fact, they are neither. The gift of tears is concerned with living in and with the truth and with the new life that the truth always brings. The tears are like the breaking of waters of the womb before the birth of a child.

Alan Jones
Soul Making

REFLECTING ON YOUR LIFE

Reading the Moment

Reflecting on the Moment

Is there any passage of Scripture that comes to mind that sheds light on this moment?

Responding to the Moment

Reaching up prayerfully

Reaching out personally

You will be sorrowful, but your sorrow will be turned to joy. Whenever a woman is in travail she has sorrow, because her hour has come; but when she gives birth to the child, she remembers the anguish no more, for joy that a child has been born into the world. *(John 16:20b-21)*

MOMENTS OF THE PAST

In his book, *Searching for Memory*, Harvard professor Daniel L. Schacter talks about the moments of the past and how they shape us. "Memory is a central part of the brain's attempt to make sense of experience, and to tell coherent stories about it. These tales are all we have of our pasts, and so they are potent determinants of how we view ourselves and what we do. Yet our stories are built from different ingredients: snippets of what actually happened, thoughts about what might have happened, and beliefs that guide us as we attempt to remember. Our memories are fragile but powerful products of what we recall from the past, believe about the present, and imagine about the future."

Throughout the Bible we are exhorted to remember the past. The Israelites are called to remember the way the Lord freed them from slavery in Egypt (Deuteronomy 8:11-14). The church is called to remember Jesus and the way He freed us from slavery to sin (Luke 22:19). We are called to remember Christ's life as an example to follow (Hebrews 12:3) and Lot's wife as an example not to (Luke 17:32). Part of the ministry of the Holy Spirit has to do with helping us to remember (John 14:26). And when Jesus came to the two disciples on the Emmaus Road, His primary purpose in coming was to help them remember some of the things they had forgotten (Luke 24:13-27).

The deeds of the past and the words of the past exist in our memory for a purpose. What was said there and done there, either by us or to us, can be a blessing or a curse, depending on how we view them.

Faith that God is sovereign is an essential lens in viewing the past. When Joseph looked back over the painful memories of what his brothers had done to him, he was able to say, "You meant evil against me, but God meant it for good . . ." (Genesis 50:20). He could say that only because he viewed his past from the wide-angle lens of God's perspective instead of through the narrow lens of his own.

168

Forgiveness is the other lens necessary in viewing the past. Again, we turn to the example of Joseph. He could have believed in the sovereignty of God but still have punished his brothers for what they had done. But he didn't. The Scriptures tell us that when his brothers fell down before him, Joseph said, " 'Do not be afraid, for am I in God's place? As for you, you meant evil against me, but God meant it for good in order to bring about this present result to preserve many people alive. So therefore, do not be afraid; I will provide for you and your little ones.' So he comforted them and spoke kindly to them" (Genesis 50:19-21). Forgiveness is what freed Joseph from being enslaved to the past, guarding his heart from bitterness and giving him the opportunity to restore his relationship with his brothers.

Faith and forgiveness are essential when looking back on your life. So is gratitude. For good things happened in the past, too. And good things were said. Those things are to be remembered as well, understood maybe for the first time for what they really were—precious gifts that helped us become who we are today.

As you work your way through the next section of the journal, pray for the Holy Spirit to bring moments from the past to your remembrance. Read the moment and reflect on it with a new set of glasses. And see if God doesn't prompt you to respond in some very specific ways.

Date *Sat., April 5, 1997*

You are told a lot about your education, but some beautiful, sacred memory, preserved since childhood, is perhaps the best education of all. If a man carries many such memories into life with him, he is saved for the rest of his days. And even if only one good memory is left in our hearts, it may also be the instrument of our salvation one day.

Fyodor Dostoyevsky

The Brothers Karamazov

From the Epilogue, Vol. 2, Set 3

REFLECTING ON YOUR LIFE

Reading the Moment

I had gone with my brother to McKinney, Texas for a book signing and afterwards we went to a nursing home to visit Ruth Wilson, a 99-year old woman who was a close friend of my parents when they lived there from 1946-1948. My dad had been a football coach there and had coached the Wilson's two boys, Jim and Paul. I wasn't born until 1950, but some of my earliest and best childhood memories were of our yearly family trip to visit some of the people my parents knew while they lived in McKinney. The Wilsons were always one of our stops. Ruth was always so kind to all of us kids, letting us play in their attic, and hugging us, smiling at us. She was now weak and frail and could hardly hear. You either had to talk loudly in her left ear or write what you wanted to say on paper.

Reflecting on the Moment

My brother and I went by the Wilson's old house, where the grandkids had been boxing up all of Ruth's belongings. They graciously let us come in and look around. Room by room all the pleasant memories of the Wilson's love and hospitality came back to us. As we talked on the way home, we realized what a profound effect those dozen or so trips there had on us. We were just kids. And yet we were more than that. We were adults in-the-making. And part of what went into the making was the kindness shown us by all of the Wilson family. It made me realize, that day we spent there, how important it is to be kind to children, to leave in their memory a clear picture that they are loved and treasured and special.

Is there any passage of Scripture that comes to mind that sheds light on this moment?

Whoever receives one such child in my name receives Me. (Matt. 18:5)

Responding to the Moment

Reaching up prayerfully

Thank you, God, for the Wilsons of McKinney and for how kind and gracious they always were to us kids. We never felt we were an inconvenience or in the way. We were always made to feel not only welcome but cherished. What a gift they gave us. God, bless them for blessing us. And help me to pass on that blessing to those kids who are growing up around me and who visit our home over the years.

Reaching out personally

Make it a point to reach out to every kid who comes to our house, whether it's a friend of one of our children or the child of one of our friends. Give them the space to play and be kids. Give them good food, lots of hugs, and talk with them and listen to what they have to say. Bless them the way the Wilsons blessed me.

I am mindful of the sincere faith within you, which first dwelt in your grandmother Lois, and your mother Eunice, and I am sure that it is in you as well.

Continue in the things you have learned and become convinced of, knowing from whom you have learned them; and that from childhood you have known the sacred writings which are able to give you the wisdom that leads to salvation through faith which is in Christ Jesus. *(2 Timothy 1:5; 3:14-15)*

Date

Memory! What a gift of God. And what a tragedy at times. Memory can be of horrible things one wants to forget, coming at times like a nightmare bringing trembling and horror, or memory can be of wonderful things one enjoys living and reliving. Memory can bring sudden understanding later in life when things suddenly fall into place and you realize what was happening, and memory can give you courage to go on—just when it is needed. Memory can quiet in time of turmoil or can transport one out of the danger of being plunged into something false. Memory can suddenly become so vivid as to stop a person from doing something wrong—because of the unmistakable contrast being flashed on the screen of the mind—and memory can cause someone to be compassionate to another in need, whose need would not have been noticed had it not been linked in the mind's picture with a deep experience in the past which prepared an understanding.

Edith Schaeffer
What Is a Family?

REFLECTING ON YOUR LIFE

Reading the Moment

Reflecting on the Moment

Is there any passage of Scripture that comes to mind that sheds light on this moment?

Responding to the Moment

Reaching up prayerfully

Reaching out personally

If you should say in your heart, "These nations are greater than I; how can I dispossess them?" you shall not be afraid of them; you shall well remember what the Lord your God did to Pharaoh and to all Egypt: the great trials which your eyes saw and the signs and the wonders and the mighty hand and the outstretched arm by which the Lord your God brought you out. So shall the Lord your God do to all the peoples of whom you are afraid. *(Deuteronomy 7:17-19)*

Know, then, that it is not because of your righteousness that the Lord your God is giving you this good land to possess, for you are a stubborn people. Remember, do not forget how you provoked the Lord your God to wrath in the wilderness; from the day that you left the land of Egypt until you arrived at this place, you have been rebellious against the Lord. Even at Horeb you provoked the Lord to wrath, and the Lord was so angry with you that He would have destroyed you. *(Deuteronomy 9:6-8)*

Date

Each childhood wound and every spiritual teaching has been presented to help us cultivate a particular aspect of mercy and compassion toward ourselves. At each juncture we
have been confronted with a choice: Do we meet ourselves and our wounds with judgment or with mercy? Do we touch our childhood memories with anger, or soften them
with love and forgiveness? Do we recall our violations with shame, or embrace them with
genuine acceptance; do we react with fear and isolation, or with faith and courage? Do
we add to the violence within ourselves, or do we cultivate unconditional love and kindness for all we have been and all we have become?

Wayne Muller

Legacy of the Heart: The Spiritual Advantages of a Painful Childhood

REFLECTING ON YOUR LIFE

Reading the Moment

Reflecting on the Moment

Is there any passage of Scripture that comes to mind that sheds light on this
moment?

Responding to the Moment

Reaching up prayerfully

Reaching out personally

When Joseph's brothers saw that their father was dead, they said, "What if Joseph should bear a grudge against us and pay us back in full for all the wrong which we did to him!" So they sent a message to Joseph, saying, "Your father charged before he died, saying, 'Thus you shall say to Joseph, "Please forgive, I beg you, the transgression of your brothers and their sin, for they did you wrong."' And now, please forgive the transgression of the servants of the God of your father."

And Joseph wept when they spoke to him.

Then his brothers also came and fell down before him and said, "Behold, we are your servants."

But Joseph said to them, "Do not be afraid, for am I in God's place? And as for you, you meant evil against me, but God meant it for good in order to bring about this present result, to preserve many people alive." *(Genesis 50:15-20)*

Date

One way or another, we are always remembering, of course. There is no escaping it even if we want to, or at least no escaping it for long, though God knows there are times when we try to, don't want to remember. In one sense the past is dead and gone, but in another sense, it is of course not done with at all or at least not done with us. Every person we have ever known, every place we have ever seen, everything that has ever happened to us—it all lives and breathes deep in us somewhere whether we like it or not, and sometimes it doesn't take much to bring it back to the surface in bits and pieces. A scrap of some song that was popular years ago. A book we read as a child. A stretch of road we used to travel. An old photograph, an old letter. There is no telling what trivial thing may do it, and then suddenly there it all is—something that happened to us once—and it is there not just as a picture on the wall to stand back from and gaze at but as a reality we are so much a part of still and that is still so much a part of us that we feel with something close to its original intensity and freshness what it felt like, say, to fall in love at the age of sixteen, or to smell the smells and hear the sounds of a house that has long since disappeared, or to laugh till the tears ran down our cheeks with somebody who died more years ago than we can easily count or for whom, in every way that matters, we might as well have died years ago ourselves. Old failures, old hurts. Times too beautiful to tell or too terrible. Memories come at us helter-skelter and unbidden, sometimes so thick and fast that they are more than we can handle in their poignance, sometimes so sparsely that we all but cry out to remember more.

Frederick Buechner
A Room Called Remember

REFLECTING ON YOUR LIFE

Reading the Moment

Reflecting on the Moment

Is there any passage of Scripture that comes to mind that sheds light on this moment?

Responding to the Moment

Reaching up prayerfully

Reaching out personally

By the rivers of Babylon,
There we sat down and wept,
When we remembered Zion.
Upon the willows in the midst of it
We hung our harps.
For there our captors demanded of us songs,
And our tormentors mirth, saying,
"Sing us one of the songs of Zion."

(Psalm 137:1-3)

Date

Recall the pain of being wronged, the hurt of being stung, cheated, demeaned. Doesn't the memory of it fuel the fire of fury again, reheat the pain again, make it hurt again? Suppose you never forgive, suppose you feel the hurt each time your memory lights on the people who did you wrong. And suppose you have a compulsion to think of them constantly. You have become a prisoner of your past pain; you are locked into a torture chamber of your own making. Time should have left your pain behind; but you keep it alive to let it flay at you over and over.

Your own memory is a replay of your hurt—a videotape within your soul that plays unending reruns of your old rendezvous with pain. You cannot switch it off. You are hooked into it like a pain junkie; you become addicted to your remembrance of pain past. You are lashed again each time your memory spins the tape. Is this fair to yourself— this wretched justice of not forgiving? You could not be more unfair to yourself.

The only way to heal the pain that will not heal itself is to forgive the person who hurt you. Forgiving stops the reruns of pain. Forgiving heals your memory as you change your memory's vision.

Lewis Smedes
Forgive & Forget

REFLECTING ON YOUR LIFE

Reading the Moment

Reflecting on the Moment

Is there any passage of Scripture that comes to mind that sheds light on this moment?

Responding to the Moment

Reaching up prayerfully

Reaching out personally

For if you forgive men for their transgressions, your heavenly Father will also forgive you. But if you do not forgive men, then your Father will not forgive your transgressions. *(Matthew 6:14-15)*

Date

The Kilns, 6 July 63

Dear Mary

. . . Do you know, only a few weeks ago I realised suddenly that I at last had forgiven the cruel schoolmaster who so darkened my childhood. I'd been trying to do it for years; and like you, each time I thought I'd done it, I found, after a week or so it all had to be attempted over again. But this time I feel sure it is the real thing. And (like learning to swim or to ride a bicycle) the moment it does happen it seems so easy and you wonder why on earth you didn't do it years ago.

Yours, Jack

C.S. Lewis
Letters to an American Lady

REFLECTING ON YOUR LIFE

Reading the Moment

Reflecting on the Moment

Is there any passage of Scripture that comes to mind that sheds light on this moment?

Responding to the Moment

Reaching up prayerfully

Reaching out personally

Let all bitterness and wrath and anger and clamor and slander be put away from you, along with all malice. And be kind to one another, tender-hearted, forgiving each other, just as God in Christ also has forgiven you. (*Ephesians 4:31-32*)

MOMENTS OF GOD'S SILENCE

It is the nature of God to speak.

It is also the nature of God to speak in a variety of different ways.

In times past He has spoken through prophets and priests, kings and commoners, natural disasters and international wars, through the written word and the spoken word, through dreams and visions, signs and wonders, angels and animals, through the handwriting on a wall and the handwriting on our hearts.

Though it is His nature to speak, sometimes God is silent. And maybe the purpose of His silence is to give resonance to the words He has already spoken to you or to me. Or maybe He is simply waiting for us to trust and obey what He has already revealed to us before He reveals anything else.

The pattern of biblical revelation is something like the way the revelation came to Ray Kinsella in the movie *Field of Dreams.* It was only after he responded to the words, "If you build it, he will come," that he was given the next bit of revelation he needed. And it was only after he responded to the next bit of revelation that he was given another bit. Take, for example, the revelation Saul received on the road to Damascus (Acts 9). It came in fragments. First came the revelation from Christ, telling him to "rise, and enter the city, and it shall be told you what you must do" (v. 6). When Saul obeyed that bit of revelation, Ananias was sent to the city to restore his sight (vv. 10-19). Later Saul was commissioned by the Holy Spirit to preach the gospel to the Gentile world (13:3).

The silence of God can be a devastating thing. But maybe, even through His silence, God is saying something, just as through our silence in a conversation we too are saying something.

Maybe the silence is saying, "I'm giving your words my full attention, and I want to hear everything you have to say before I respond."

Maybe the silence is saying that "now is not the appropriate time to say anything." Maybe the silence means that "whatever I have to say, if I said it now,

182

wouldn't be understood . . . or received . . . or fully appreciated."

Maybe the silence means that "I'm waiting for you to say something else before I speak. Maybe I'm wanting you to come to some conclusions on your own instead of Me spelling it out for you."

Or maybe the silence means "I'm just wanting you to hear so badly that I'm using the silence to heighten your attention so that when I do speak, you will hear every word."

Take some time to examine the silence of God in your own experience. You might want to reflect on some protracted period of silence in the past or the silence you may be presently experiencing. The best you can, try to hear some echo of God's voice in those silences.

Date *Summer, 1997*

Meanwhile, where is God? This is one of the most disquieting symptoms. When you are happy, so happy that you have no sense of needing Him, so happy that you are tempted to feel His claims upon you as an interruption, if you remember yourself and turn to Him with gratitude and praise, you will be—or so it feels—welcomed with open arms. But go to Him when your need is desperate, when all other help is vain, and what do you find? A door slammed in your face, and a sound of bolting and double bolting on the inside. After that, silence. You may as well turn away. The longer you wait, the more emphatic the silence will become. There are no lights in the windows. It might be an empty house. Was it ever inhabited? It seemed so once. And that seeming was as strong as this. What can this mean? Why is He so present a commander in our time of prosperity and so very absent a help in time of trouble?

C.S. Lewis
A Grief Observed

REFLECTING ON YOUR LIFE

Reading the Moment

It is a moment at the Palmer Lake Reservoir, a lake in the mountains that is about a 30-minute hike from my office. I have been praying for sometime, as I am praying today, about my career. It is a confusing and somewhat discouraging time. I've tried to listen in prayer, in the circumstances of my life, in the Scriptures, and in the counsel of other people, but so far God seems silent. It feels like the changing of seasons, that uncomfortable transition between the death of something and the birth of something else, but I can't tell for sure. I pray as I look at the sky and call out to God for answer, but I get no answer.

Reflecting on the Moment

As I'm sitting there, a bundle of anxiety, I seem in such contrast to everything around me. The water is calm. The trees, tall and quiet. The huge boulders, stoic. The clouds above slowly, almost imperceptibly, moving. It's as if all of nature is joining together in one chorus, singing ever-so-softly one word — Relax. Everything there is at rest. Rooted. Growing. Standing. Sailing. All in their own time. All under God's care. A season comes, a season goes. A tree falls down. A thousand others sprout. The snow melts and fills the reservoir. The reservoir filters into the town. Everything here seems so peaceful, so at rest in the care of God. Why, O God, can't I?

Is there any passage of Scripture that comes to mind that sheds light on this moment?

Look at the birds, free and unfettered, not tied down to a job description, careless in the care of God. And you count ~~for him~~ far more to him than birds. (Matt. 6 – The Message)

Responding to the Moment

Reaching up prayerfully

Please, God, help me to listen to your voice in nature as well as in the Scripture. Help me to trust you with the rooted tenacity of the trees and the carefree winging of the birds. It all boils down to one thing. Do I trust you? ~~Really~~ trust you. Do I trust that you see me struggling, that you care, that there is some purpose to my struggles? Help me to ~~hear what~~ hear what you have to say to me through the articulate silence of nature: Relax. All in its time, my child. All in its good time.

Reaching out personally

I need to spend more time in nature and less time in the newspaper or with my organizer. I need to maybe focus on other people in my prayers, instead of so much on myself. I think that would help. Praying through some passages of Scriptures might help too. Maybe Ps. 139, Romans 8, Philippians.

To Thee, O Lord, I call;
My rock, do not be deaf to me,
Lest, if Thou be silent to me,
I become like those who go down to the pit.
Hear the voice of my supplications when I cry to Thee for help.
(Psalm 28:1-2a)

Date

The mystery of God's presence, therefore, can be touched only by a deep awareness of his absence. It is in the center of our longing for the absent God that we discover his footprints, and realize that our desire to love God is born out of the love with which he has touched us. In the patient waiting for the loved one, we discover how much he has filled our lives already. Just as the love of a mother for her son can grow deeper when he is far away, just as children can learn to appreciate their parents more when they have left the home, just as lovers can rediscover each other during long periods of absence, so our intimate relationship with God can become deeper and more mature by the purifying experience of his absence. By listening to our longings, we hear God as their creator. By touching the center of our solitude, we sense that we have been touched by loving hands. By watching carefully the endless desire to love, we come to the growing awareness that we can love only because we have been loved first, and that we can offer intimacy only because we are born out of the inner intimacy of God himself.

Henri Nouwen
Reaching Out

REFLECTING ON YOUR LIFE

Reading the Moment

Reflecting on the Moment

Is there any passage of Scripture that comes to mind that sheds light on this moment?

Responding to the Moment

Reaching up prayerfully

Reaching out personally

I was asleep, but my heart was awake.
A voice! My beloved was knocking:
"Open to me, my sister, my darling,
My dove, my perfect one!
For my head is drenched with dew,
My locks with the damp of the night."
I have taken off my dress,
How can I put it on again? . . .
My beloved extended his hand through the opening,
And my feelings were aroused for him.
I arose to open to my beloved;
And my hands dripped with myrrh,
And my fingers with liquid myrrh,
On the handles of the bolt.
I opened to my beloved,
But my beloved had turned away and had gone!
My heart went out to him as he spoke.
I searched for him, but I did not find him;
I called him, but he did not answer me.

(Song of Solomon 5:2-6)

Date

Is not a picture painted on a canvas by the application of one stroke of the brush at a time? Similarly the cruel chisel destroys a stone with each cut. But what the stone suffers by repeated blows is no less than the shape the mason is making of it. And should a poor stone be asked, "What is happening to you?", it might reply, "Don't ask me. All I know is that for my part there is nothing for me to know or do, only to remain steady under the hand of my master and to love him and suffer him to work out my destiny. It is for him to know how to achieve this. I know neither what he is doing nor why. I only know that he is doing what is best and most perfect, and I suffer each cut of the chisel as though it were the best thing for me, even though, to tell the truth, each one is my idea of ruin, destruction and defacement. But, ignoring all this, I rest contented with the present moment. Thinking only of my duty to it, I submit to the work of this skilful master without caring to know what it is."

Jean-Pierre De Caussade
The Sacrament of the Present Moment

REFLECTING ON YOUR LIFE

Reading the Moment

Reflecting on the Moment

Is there any passage of Scripture that comes to mind that sheds light on this moment?

Responding to the Moment

Reaching up prayerfully

Reaching out personally

Woe to the one who quarrels with his Maker—
An earthenware vessel among the vessels of the earth!
Will the clay say to the potter, "What are you doing?"

(Isaiah 45:9)

And we know that God causes all things to work together for good to those who love God, to those who are called according to His purpose. For whom He foreknew, He also predestined to become conformed to the image of His Son. *(Romans 8:28-29)*

Date

When I lay these questions before God I get no answer. But a rather special sort of "No answer." It is not the locked door. It is more like a silent, certainly not uncompassionate, gaze. As though He shook His head not in refusal but waiving the question. Like, "Peace, child; you don't understand."

C.S. Lewis
A Grief Observed

REFLECTING ON YOUR LIFE

Reading the Moment

Reflecting on the Moment

Is there any passage of Scripture that comes to mind that sheds light on this moment?

Responding to the Moment

Reaching up prayerfully

Reaching out personally

"The Lord is my portion," says my soul,
"Therefore I have hope in Him."
The Lord is good to those who wait for Him,
To the person who seeks Him.
It is good that he waits silently
For the salvation of the Lord.
It is good for a man that he should bear
The yoke in his youth.
Let him sit alone and be silent
Since He has laid it on him.
Let him put his mouth in the dust,
Perhaps there is hope.
Let him give his cheek to the smiter;
Let him be filled with reproach.
For the Lord will not reject forever,
For if He causes grief,
Then He will have compassion
According to His abundant lovingkindness.

(Lamentations 3:24-32)

Date

I believe that much of our religious unbelief is due to a wrong conception of and a wrong feeling for the Scriptures of Truth. A silent God suddenly began to speak in a book and when the book was finished lapsed back into silence again forever. Now we read the book as the record of what God said when He was for a brief time in a speaking mood. With notions like that in our heads how can we believe? The facts are that God is not silent, has never been silent. It is the nature of God to speak. The second Person of the Holy Trinity is called the Word.

A.W. Tozer
The Pursuit of God

REFLECTING ON YOUR LIFE

Reading the Moment

Reflecting on the Moment

Is there any passage of Scripture that comes to mind that sheds light on this moment?

Responding to the Moment

Reaching up prayerfully

Reaching out personally

In the beginning was the Word, and the Word was with God, and the Word was God. . . .

And the Word became flesh, and dwelt among us, and we beheld His glory, glory as of the only begotten from the Father, full of grace and truth. *(John 1:1, 14)*

God, after He spoke long ago to the fathers in the prophets in many portions and in many ways, in these last days has spoken to us in His Son. *(Hebrews 1:1-2a)*

Date

Love must express and communicate itself.
> That's its nature.
> When people begin to love one another,
>> they start telling everything that's happened to them,
>>> every detail of their daily life;
>> they "reveal" themselves to each other,
>>> unbosom themselves and exchange confidences.

God hasn't ceased being Revelation
> any more than He's ceased being Love.
He enjoys expressing Himself.
> Since He's Love,
>> He must give Himself,
>>> share His secrets,
>>> communicate with us
>>> and reveal Himself to anyone
>>>> who wants to listen.

Louis Evely
That Man Is You

REFLECTING ON YOUR LIFE

Reading the Moment

Reflecting on the Moment

Is there any passage of Scripture that comes to mind that sheds light on this moment?

Responding to the Moment

Reaching up prayerfully

Reaching out personally

The crooked man is an abomination to the Lord;
But He is intimate with the upright. (*Proverbs 3:32*)

He who has My commandments and keeps them, he it is who loves Me; and he who loves Me shall be loved by My Father, and I will love him, and will disclose Myself to him. (*John 14:21*)

SECTION FOURTEEN

MOMENTS OF WAITING

Just as an artist's body of work would bear certain stylistic similarities whether she worked with oil paints or watercolors, so the way God works in the natural world bears similarities to the way He works in the spiritual world.

The German poet Rilke was a student of both worlds. In a letter to a young poet, he explained that the natural process of becoming an artist was "to ripen like the tree which does not force its sap and stands confident in the storms of Spring without fear lest no Summer might come after."

To ripen, either as an artist or as a human being or as a Christian, takes time. And the greater the thing that is being grown, the more time is necessary for its ripening. Love, joy, peace, patience, kindness are all fruit of the Spirit. And they all take time to reach fruition. The only fruit that doesn't take time to produce is artificial fruit, which has neither the taste nor the nutrition of real fruit, nor the seeds to reproduce itself.

The stages to ripeness are both successive and progressive. First the seed, then the stem, then the leaf, then the bloom, then finally the fruit.

The same is true of the things we pray for. They take time. In some cases a lot of time, as George MacDonald notes: "Perhaps, indeed, the better the gift we pray for, the more time is necessary for its arrival. To give us the spiritual gift we desire, God may have to begin far back in our spirit, in regions unknown to us, and do much work that we can be aware of only in the results. . . ."

Children are one of the gifts God gives us (Psalm 127:3). The gestation period is nine months. Why so long? Because God is not only preparing a baby for the outside world, He is preparing the outside world for the baby. Month by month God is preparing a place not just in the parents' home but in their hearts. And that takes time. A lot of time. And a lot of thought . . . and conversations . . . and prayers. Even tears. They are all necessary to give the baby a nurturing environment in which to ripen as a human being.

196

To ripen from childhood to adulthood in the faith also takes time.
And faith.

The faith is not in the one who sows or in the one who waters or even in the one who waits. The faith is in the Word of God that has been planted in our heart (James 1:21), and in God who causes the growth (1 Corinthians 3:6-7), knowing that He who has begun a good work in us will oversee the growth and bring it to fruition (Philippians 1:6).

Date *Summer, 1996*

Over the infinity of space and time, the infinitely more infinite love of God comes to possess us. He comes at his own time. We have the power to consent to receive him or to refuse. If we remain deaf, he comes back again and again like a beggar, but also, like a beggar, one day he stops coming. If we consent, God puts a little seed in us and goes away again. From that moment God has no more to do; neither have we, except to wait. . . . It is not as easy as it seems, for the growth of the seed within us is painful. Moreover, from the very fact that we accept this growth, we cannot avoid destroying whatever gets in the way, pulling up the weeds, cutting the good grass, and unfortunately the good grass is part of our very flesh, so that this gardening amounts to a violent operation.

Simone Weil
Waiting for God

REFLECTING ON YOUR LIFE

Reading the Moment

It was a moment on Academy Boulevard when I was driving one day in Colorado Springs. I was thinking about my life and praying kind of a give-up prayer about ~~my~~ some of the things that I thought God had put in my heart but that had never happened. I had been praying for this one particular thing for 15 years, and I was getting a little tired, frankly, of hearing myself pray about it for so long. It was at that time that a large cream-colored truck pulled in front of me. On the back of the truck was a big green tree. And over the tree or under it (I forget which) were the words: "Tree of Life".

Reflecting on the Moment

The moment would have ~~been~~ meant nothing to me except that a few days earlier I had come across a verse in Proverbs that expressed my feelings and became my prayer. The first half of the verse goes like this: "Hope deferred makes the heart sick" (Proverbs 13:12) I prayed, "God, please. My heart is sick. I just can't keep praying and the hope keep being deferred. Please either answers my prayers or redirect my passions."

The second half of the verse is what made that moment on Academy Boulevard seem significant. It reads: "But desire fulfilled is a tree of life : Could it be that the moment was one through which God was speaking to me, encouraging me not to give up but to keep hoping, keep praying?

Is there any passage of Scripture that comes to mind that sheds light on this moment?

Hope deferred makes the heart sick,
But desire fulfilled is a tree of life.

(Prov. 13:12)

Responding to the Moment

Reaching up prayerfully

Thank you, God, for that moment on Academy ~~road~~ Boulevard. I needed it. I was so tired of praying, tired of hoping. Fifteen years is a long time. I know it's not in your scheme of things, but in mine, it's a third of my life. Help me to trust not only the seeds of passion you have planted in my heart but in your timing in bringing those seeds to fruition.

Reaching out personally

I will continue to work and pray toward the goal of what God has put in my heart. I will try not to give-up until He tells me to give up. I will do everything I can to prepare myself ~~for the moment~~ to be ready should the time come when God ~~may~~ says to me: "Yes. Now is the time." But I will do nothing to force the time.

The kingdom of God is like a man who casts seed upon the soil; and goes to bed at night and gets up by day, and the seed sprouts up and grows—how, he himself does not know. The soil produces crops by itself; first the blade, then the head, then the mature grain in the head. (*Mark 4:26-28*)

Date

Think of yourself just as a seed patiently wintering in the earth; waiting to come up a flower in the Gardener's good time, up into the real world, the real waking.

C.S. Lewis
Letter dated June 28, 1963

REFLECTING ON YOUR LIFE

Reading the Moment

Reflecting on the Moment

Is there any passage of Scripture that comes to mind that sheds light on this moment?

Responding to the Moment

Reaching up prayerfully

Reaching out personally

Truly, truly, I say to you, unless a grain of wheat falls into the earth and dies, it remains by itself alone; but if it dies, it bears much fruit. *(John 12:24)*

Date

We do not obtain the most precious gifts by going in search of them but by waiting for them.

Simone Weil
Waiting for God

REFLECTING ON YOUR LIFE

Reading the Moment

Reflecting on the Moment

Is there any passage of Scripture that comes to mind that sheds light on this moment?

Responding to the Moment

Reaching up prayerfully

Reaching out personally

And it will come about after this
That I will pour out My Spirit on all mankind;
And your sons and daughters will prophesy,
Your old men will dream dreams,
Your young men will see visions.
And even on the male and female servants
I will pour out My Spirit in those days.

(Joel 2:28-29)

And gathering them together, He commanded them not to leave Jerusalem, but to wait for what the Father had promised, "Which," He said, "you heard of from Me; for John baptized with water, but you shall be baptized with the Holy Spirit not many days from now."

(Acts 1:4-5)

And when the day of Pentecost had come, they were all together in one place. And suddenly there came from heaven a noise like a violent, rushing wind, and it filled the whole house where they were sitting. And there appeared to them tongues as of fire distributing themselves, and they rested on each one of them. And they were all filled with the Holy Spirit and began to speak with other tongues, as the Spirit was giving them utterance.

Now there were Jews living in Jerusalem, devout men, from every nation under heaven. And when this sound occurred, the multitude came together, and were bewildered, because they were each one hearing them speak in his own language. . . .

And they continued in amazement and great perplexity, saying to one another, "What does this mean?"

But others were mocking and saying, "They are full of sweet wine."

But Peter, taking his stand with the eleven, raised his voice and declared to them: "Men of Judea, and all you who live in Jerusalem, let this be known to you, and give heed to my words. For these men are not drunk, as you suppose, for it is only the third hour of the day; but this is what was spoken through the prophet Joel:

'And it shall be in the last days,' God says,
'That I will pour forth of My Spirit upon all mankind;
And your sons and your daughters shall prophesy,
And your young men shall see visions,
And your old men shall dream dreams;
Even upon My bondslaves, both men and women,
I will in those days pour forth of My Spirit.

(Acts 2:1-6, 12-18)

Date

Picture a blazing hot forge and a piece of gold thrust into it to be heated until all that is impure and false is burnt out. As it is heated, it is also softened and shaped by the metalworker. Our faith is the gold; our suffering is the fire. The forge is the waiting: it is the tension and longing and, at times, anguish of waiting for God to keep his promises.

Ben Patterson

Waiting

REFLECTING ON YOUR LIFE

Reading the Moment

Reflecting on the Moment

Is there any passage of Scripture that comes to mind that sheds light on this moment?

Responding to the Moment

Reaching up prayerfully

Reaching out personally

In this you greatly rejoice, even though now for a little while, if necessary, you have been distressed by various trials, that the proof of your faith, being more precious than gold which is perishable, even though tested by fire, may be found to result in praise and glory and honor at the revelation of Jesus Christ. (*1 Peter 1:6-7*)

Date

The fullness of one's soul evolves slowly. We're asked to go within to gestate the newness God is trying to form; we're asked to collaborate with grace.

That doesn't mean that grace isn't a gift. Nor does it mean that the deliberate process of waiting produces grace. But waiting does provide the time and space necessary for grace to happen. Spirit needs a container to pour itself into. Grace needs an arena in which to incarnate. Waiting can be such a place, if we allow it.

Sue Monk Kidd
When the Heart Waits

REFLECTING ON YOUR LIFE

Reading the Moment

Reflecting on the Moment

Is there any passage of Scripture that comes to mind that sheds light on this moment?

Responding to the Moment

Reaching up prayerfully

Reaching out personally

Now Jesus loved Martha, and her sister, and Lazarus. When therefore He heard that he was sick, He then stayed two days longer in the place where He was. . . . After that He said to them, "Our friend Lazarus has fallen asleep; but I go, that I may awaken him out of sleep. . . . Lazarus is dead, and I am glad for your sakes that I was not there, so that you may believe, but let us go to him." *(John 11:5-6, 11, 14-15)*

Date

Waiting is not just the thing we have to do until we get what we hope for. Waiting is part of the process of becoming what we hope for.

Ben Patterson
Waiting

REFLECTING ON YOUR LIFE

Reading the Moment

Reflecting on the Moment

Is there any passage of Scripture that comes to mind that sheds light on this moment?

Responding to the Moment

Reaching up prayerfully

Reaching out personally

The Lord is good to those who wait for Him,
To the person who seeks Him.
It is good that he waits silently
For the salvation of the Lord.

(Lamentations 3:25-26)

CONCLUSION

This journal was designed to help you become more spiritually sensitive to the everyday moments of your life. God may speak to you through other moments than I have suggested, for the moments I have chosen are merely representative, not exhaustive.

I hope that by working your way through the journal you have entered into a more meaningful relationship with the world around you, experiencing it on a deeper and richer level. I especially hope it has helped you discern the voice of God in the circumstances of your life, experiencing Him on a deeper and richer level, too.

In my own relationship with Him, I have found He speaks to me more from the vocabulary of my own experience, with images that are both near to me and dear to me. Maybe you experienced something like that as well.

The way God speaks to us by and large is, I think, the way a mother speaks to her young child. The mother doesn't speak to the child through the Latin she learned in college but through lullabies.

Through the embrace of her arms and the nourishment of her breast.

Through the inflections in her voice and the music box she has put by the crib.

Through her presence when the baby cries and her absence when it sleeps.

Through all of these things, sometimes verbal, sometimes nonverbal, the mother's love is communicated.

So is the love of God.

For it is the nature of love to express itself.

And God loves us so much that He sent His Son, the very Word of God, not only to die for us but to be with us . . . and to speak with us.

OPEN TOPIC SECTION

REFLECTING ON YOUR LIFE

Date

Reading the Moment

Reflecting on the Moment

Is there any passage of Scripture that comes to mind that sheds light on this moment?

Responding to the Moment

Reaching up prayerfully

Reaching out personally

REFLECTING ON YOUR LIFE

Date

Reading the Moment

Reflecting on the Moment

Is there any passage of Scripture that comes to mind that sheds light on this moment?

Responding to the Moment

Reaching up prayerfully

Reaching out personally

REFLECTING ON YOUR LIFE

Date

Reading the Moment

Reflecting on the Moment

Is there any passage of Scripture that comes to mind that sheds light on this moment?

Responding to the Moment

Reaching up prayerfully

Reaching out personally

REFLECTING ON YOUR LIFE

Date

Reading the Moment

Reflecting on the Moment

Is there any passage of Scripture that comes to mind that sheds light on this moment?

Responding to the Moment

Reaching up prayerfully

Reaching out personally

REFLECTING ON YOUR LIFE

Date

Reading the Moment

Reflecting on the Moment

Is there any passage of Scripture that comes to mind that sheds light on this moment?

Responding to the Moment

Reaching up prayerfully

Reaching out personally

REFLECTING ON YOUR LIFE

Date

Reading the Moment

Reflecting on the Moment

Is there any passage of Scripture that comes to mind that sheds light on this moment?

Responding to the Moment

Reaching up prayerfully

Reaching out personally

REFLECTING ON YOUR LIFE

Date

Reading the Moment

Reflecting on the Moment

Is there any passage of Scripture that comes to mind that sheds light on this moment?

Responding to the Moment

Reaching up prayerfully

Reaching out personally

REFLECTING ON YOUR LIFE

Date

Reading the Moment

Reflecting on the Moment

Is there any passage of Scripture that comes to mind that sheds light on this moment?

Responding to the Moment

Reaching up prayerfully

Reaching out personally

REFLECTING ON YOUR LIFE

Date

Reading the Moment

Reflecting on the Moment

Is there any passage of Scripture that comes to mind that sheds light on this moment?

Responding to the Moment

Reaching up prayerfully

Reaching out personally

REFLECTING ON YOUR LIFE

Date

Reading the Moment

Reflecting on the Moment

Is there any passage of Scripture that comes to mind that sheds light on this moment?

Responding to the Moment

Reaching up prayerfully

Reaching out personally

REFLECTING ON YOUR LIFE

Date

Reading the Moment

Reflecting on the Moment

Is there any passage of Scripture that comes to mind that sheds light on this moment?

Responding to the Moment

Reaching up prayerfully

Reaching out personally

REFLECTING ON YOUR LIFE

Date

Reading the Moment

Reflecting on the Moment

Is there any passage of Scripture that comes to mind that sheds light on this moment?

Responding to the Moment

Reaching up prayerfully

Reaching out personally

REFLECTING ON YOUR LIFE

Date

Reading the Moment

Reflecting on the Moment

Is there any passage of Scripture that comes to mind that sheds light on this moment?

Responding to the Moment

Reaching up prayerfully

Reaching out personally

REFLECTING ON YOUR LIFE

Date

Reading the Moment

Reflecting on the Moment

Is there any passage of Scripture that comes to mind that sheds light on this moment?

Responding to the Moment

Reaching up prayerfully

Reaching out personally

REFLECTING ON YOUR LIFE

Date

Reading the Moment

Reflecting on the Moment

Is there any passage of Scripture that comes to mind that sheds light on this moment?

Responding to the Moment

Reaching up prayerfully

Reaching out personally

REFLECTING ON YOUR LIFE

Date

Reading the Moment

Reflecting on the Moment

Is there any passage of Scripture that comes to mind that sheds light on this moment?

Responding to the Moment

Reaching up prayerfully

Reaching out personally

REFLECTING ON YOUR LIFE

Date

Reading the Moment

Reflecting on the Moment

Is there any passage of Scripture that comes to mind that sheds light on this moment?

Responding to the Moment

Reaching up prayerfully

Reaching out personally

REFLECTING ON YOUR LIFE

Date

Reading the Moment

Reflecting on the Moment

Is there any passage of Scripture that comes to mind that sheds light on this moment?

Responding to the Moment

Reaching up prayerfully

Reaching out personally

REFLECTING ON YOUR LIFE

Date

Reading the Moment

Reflecting on the Moment

Is there any passage of Scripture that comes to mind that sheds light on this moment?

Responding to the Moment

Reaching up prayerfully

Reaching out personally

REFLECTING ON YOUR LIFE

Date

Reading the Moment

Reflecting on the Moment

Is there any passage of Scripture that comes to mind that sheds light on this moment?

Responding to the Moment

Reaching up prayerfully

Reaching out personally

REFLECTING ON YOUR LIFE

Date

Reading the Moment

Reflecting on the Moment

Is there any passage of Scripture that comes to mind that sheds light on this moment?

Responding to the Moment

Reaching up prayerfully

Reaching out personally

REFLECTING ON YOUR LIFE

Date

Reading the Moment

Reflecting on the Moment

Is there any passage of Scripture that comes to mind that sheds light on this moment?

Responding to the Moment

Reaching up prayerfully

Reaching out personally

REFLECTING ON YOUR LIFE

Date

Reading the Moment

Reflecting on the Moment

Is there any passage of Scripture that comes to mind that sheds light on this moment?

Responding to the Moment

Reaching up prayerfully

Reaching out personally

REFLECTING ON YOUR LIFE

Date

Reading the Moment

Reflecting on the Moment

Is there any passage of Scripture that comes to mind that sheds light on this moment?

Responding to the Moment

Reaching up prayerfully

Reaching out personally

REFLECTING ON YOUR LIFE

Date

Reading the Moment

Reflecting on the Moment

Is there any passage of Scripture that comes to mind that sheds light on this moment?

Responding to the Moment

Reaching up prayerfully

Reaching out personally

REFLECTING ON YOUR LIFE

Date

Reading the Moment

Reflecting on the Moment

Is there any passage of Scripture that comes to mind that sheds light on this moment?

Responding to the Moment

Reaching up prayerfully

Reaching out personally

REFLECTING ON YOUR LIFE

Date

Reading the Moment

Reflecting on the Moment

Is there any passage of Scripture that comes to mind that sheds light on this moment?

Responding to the Moment

Reaching up prayerfully

Reaching out personally

REFLECTING ON YOUR LIFE

Date

Reading the Moment

Reflecting on the Moment

Is there any passage of Scripture that comes to mind that sheds light on this moment?

Responding to the Moment

Reaching up prayerfully

Reaching out personally

ACKNOWLEDGMENTS

Reasonable care has been taken to trace ownership of the materials quoted from this book, and to obtain permission to use copyrighted materials, when necessary.

The Pilgrim's Regress, C.S. Lewis, 1943, Wm. B. Eerdmans Publishing Co., Grand Rapids, Michigan. All rights reserved.

The Practice of the Presence of God, Brother Lawrence, 1958, Baker Book House, Grand Rapids, Michigan. All rights reserved.

The Pursuit of God, A.W. Tozer, 1982, Christian Publishing, Camp Hill, Pennsylvania. All rights reserved.

Reaching Out, Henri Nouwen, 1975 by Henri J.M. Nouwen. Used by permission of Doubleday, a division of Bantam Doubleday Dell Publishing Group, Inc.